GREENER PASTURES

*An
Incredible
Journey
from the
Farm
to the
Fairways*

ROBERT LANDERS
AND RUSS PATE

GREENER
PASTURES

Published by Harvest Media, Inc.
820 N. Main • Fort Worth, Texas 76106

ISBN 0-9646738-0-0

*Dedicated to anyone who ever took a shag bag,
and a few golf clubs, and went to the park.*

*This book is also dedicated to Robert Wayne Landers, Sr., in loving
memory of Ceila McDaniel Landers, and to Roy Hill Pate.*

"Nothing happens unless first a dream."

— *Carl Sandburg*

GREENER
PASTURES

Contents

GREENER
PASTURES

Acknowledgments

The authors wish to thank the family and friends of Robert Landers for their support. We especially appreciate the assistance provided by Frank Anglim, Bob Buckel, Steve Champion, Don Dodgen, Ronnie Feemster, Carl Fisher, Keith Flatt, Jeffrey Fried, Kathleen Fulton,Steve Henton, Don Hood, Pat Hudson, Wayne Landers, Robert W. Landers III, Adam Lenkin, Phil Lumsden, Tommy McDaniel, Leroy Pearson, David Sann, Roland Sparks, Britt Todd and Barbee Landers Walker.

Special thanks to Monica Reeves, a terrific editor and editorial advisor, who helped shape the narrative, and to Katie Callahan, who offered editorial counsel.

This project would not have been possible without the drive and determination of Jerry Hamilton and Freddie Stewart Landers, each of whom we thank deeply.

Finally, a word of heartfelt appreciation to Daniel Collins, of Harvest Media, Inc. in Fort Worth, and Tom Keffer, of Pelican Press in Dallas, for their encouragement and inspiration, as well as their unqualified enthusiasm for seeing that Robert Landers' amazing golf saga is fully told.

GREENER
PASTURES

Foreword
by Chi Chi Rodriquez

If you watch and follow Robert Landers, I believe you will feel as I do that he is an excellent role model for both kids and adults. The way he conducts himself and the quality of his values sets, what I consider to be, the standard for courtesy and consideration to others. We need more people in the world like him.

Robert Landers is a man's man. He is a man who has worked hard all his life with very little to show for it. There's one way that God rewards poor people for all their efforts and that is by giving them physical strength. Robert has incredibly strong hands and forearms, which he developed through years of hard work on the farm, and he puts that strength to use in his golf game.

I hope that Robert will do well on the Senior PGA Tour because he's a dreamer—and America is a country where people have the opportunity to attain their dreams. In other countries of the world, people often see their dreams turn into nightmares. That's because they don't live in a democratic, or free enterprise system like America's, which allows people to realize their full potential as individuals.

With Robert, you can look into his eyes and see the whole story. You can tell that he is not a person who is jealous or envious of anyone. You can also see that he is a man on a mission to succeed.

Robert reminds me in many ways of the pioneers of America, the people who conquered then settled this country, but made no great gains monetarily. Yet these were the people who established the values and standards by which America has survived—and thrived.

Robert Landers' story is a remarkable one of courage, determination and achievement despite great odds. How could anyone not immediately be attracted to him and his wife, Freddie? How could anyone not be pulling for them? They are tender, kind-hearted, good-natured souls. Seeing them together, holding hands, is a beautiful sight.

If Robert Landers were to win a tournament in 1995, it would be one of the greatest stories—if not the greatest story—in the history of the Senior PGA Tour. I know I'm just one of many people in his corner wishing him the best.

I probably have a special feeling for Robert because I understand farming. I used to help my father with some farming back home in Puerto Rico, and I know first hand the hard work and sacrifices involved. Deep in my heart, I believe no one is more deserving of this new-found success than Robert.

If you're trying to find out what America is all about, you don't have to look much farther than Robert Landers. He is a great symbol for this country and its heritage. His remarkable story goes to show that if you work hard, and have faith in yourself, one day you'll find that your dreams can come true.

Chapter One

WE'RE NOT IN AZLE ANYMORE

My first round in my first tournament in my first season as a full-fledged member of the Senior PGA Tour and I only shoot 75. Holy cow! Well, at least I didn't do anything really embarrassing, like playing out of turn or hitting the wrong ball.

I can't say exactly what number I was hoping for, but it sure wasn't any 75. I went the whole, first round of the Royal Caribbean Classic without making a single birdie, and I didn't really hit my iron shots close enough to give myself many good birdie chances. I just never got comfortable with the speed of the greens at the Links at Key Biscayne.

Guys in the locker room were saying that these were some of the fastest greens that we would face all year. I hoped they were right. One thing was certain, these greens were a lot faster, and a lot harder to read, than the ones I was accustomed to seeing at the muny courses I play on around Fort Worth and back in Azle, my hometown. But it's like my wife, Freddie, and I tell each other all the time: We're not in Azle any more.

We haven't been in Azle, or at least not like we were before, ever since I qualified for the 1995 Senior PGA Tour in November 1994 down in Tampa. When I won playing privileges for the

1995 season, finishing in a tie for sixth to earn one of the eight fully exempt spots, the golf writers and then the whole U.S. sports media went wild over the story of how a Texas farmer wearing tennis shoes and using homemade golf clubs had come from nowhere to qualify for the Senior PGA Tour.

Freddie's and my life, ever since then, has seemed like a fairy tale. You might say we've been living the Cinderella story. Articles about us have appeared in *Sports Illustrated* and *Golf World* and all kinds of local and national newspapers. CNN News taped a feature story on us at our farm, and there was a camera crew from Connie Chung's CBS network show, "Eye To Eye," following us around for weeks. We had so many newspeople out to the farm in December and January, that I lost track of them all.

Our lives have been the focus of a media frenzy for the past three months, and while we try to be helpful and accommodating to everyone, to be honest, I like things a lot better when I can just concentrate on playing golf and not have to worry about whether the next interview is with Jim Kelly on ESPN, Dick Schaap on ABC Sports or Norm Hitzges on KLIF-AM radio, back in Dallas.

I didn't have any time to practice when my first Senior PGA Tour round was over, as I normally would have. We headed out to a party that evening that Raymond Floyd and his wife, Maria, were hosting for the Senior PGA Tour players. Freddie and I rode over to the Floyds' in a car with Tommy Aaron and Tommy and Kathy Aycock.

When we arrived at the Floyds, I suppose we felt a little like the Jed Clampetts first showing up in Beverly Hills. The Floyds have one of those big, beautiful mansions, like a castle you might see in the picture shows. I guess their home in a way shows just how much money you can make in professional golf, if you're a big winner and top gun like Raymond Floyd is.

At the party, Freddie and I met many of the Tour players for the first time. Several of the caddies, including Ray Floyd's, were shooting pool and they insisted I join them for a game.

Afterwards, when we went outside and approached the buffet table set up by the pool, Tom Wargo and his wife, Irene, came over and said, "Come on, you're going with us." Just then, Kathy Aycock said, "Come here, we have a couple chairs at the table for you."

Suddenly Freddie and I were being torn in two directions, and we didn't quite know what to do. We didn't want anyone to feel that we were choosing Tom Wargo over Tommy Aycock, which wasn't true at all. It was as if we were caught in the middle, and, not knowing etiquette or how to do social things very well, we felt a little funny, I guess. Fortunately, Kathy Aycock said, "No problem. Go right on." That made us feel really good. Then she added, "But hurry up and eat, because we're going to be leaving pretty soon."

When we sat down at the table with the Wargoes, Raymond Floyd came over and said hello and sat down; so did Jim Colbert and his wife, Marcia. Everyone was really warm and friendly and made us feel right at home. We had fun, but didn't overstay our welcome.

WE'RE AS CONTENT AS THE COWS, AS HAPPY AS ANY PEOPLE HAVE A RIGHT TO BE.

Earlier in the week, when I had been hitting practice balls on the range and Freddie was seated in the bleachers watching, Tom Wargo walked right up to her and extended his hand.

"You don't have to introduce yourself to me," said Freddie. "I know who you are. I've seen you on TV."

"Well, I know who you are," Tom told her. "I've seen you on TV, too."

That was pretty hard for us to believe, that anyone would recognize us from TV. Freddie and I live a quiet, simple, peaceful life on our 73-acre farm outside of Azle. We're as content as the cows, as happy as any people have a right to be. But after all the publicity about my qualifying for the 1995 Senior PGA Tour, which amazed even us, suddenly we're not the nobodies we used to be. It really has been a miracle.

We arrived in Miami on Saturday, January 28. We drove down from Texas with Roland Sparks, and a golf buddy of mine from Azle, in his Dodge van. The hardest part of the trip was listening to the gospel music stations Roland kept tuning in on the radio. That gospel music sounded a lot like rock-and-roll to me.

As soon as I earned my Tour card last November, Roland called and volunteered to caddy for me on Tour. I told him, "All right, if you want the job, you can have first shot at it." I was getting letters and calls from all over, so I was glad that Roland volunteered. I told myself that was one more decision out of the way.

Roland and I have played golf together for six or seven years, usually a two or three times a year in partner-type events, so he's pretty familiar with my game. He plays golf all the time, probably about an 8-handicap or so, and he's pretty good at reading putts. I'm paying him $400 week and 7 percent of whatever tournament prize money I win, but I might have to pay him a little extra to lose that gospel music.

We stopped briefly in Dothan, Alabama, where I was going to play in a two-day tournament, until the first day got rained out. Then we went on to Tampa, where I played a couple practice rounds at TPC of Tampa Bay. That's the course where I qualified for the 1995 Senior Tour, so we had a lot of happy memories from about eleven weeks earlier. Tampa is one of the early stops on the 1995 Senior PGA Tour, and I wanted to get a sneak preview of the conditions.

Then we drove down to Orlando and stopped at the PGA Merchandise Show, where we met with Jerry Hamilton, a golfing buddy of mine from Mineral Wells, Texas, who is acting as my business manager now. Jerry had lined up appointments for us with several equipment manufacturers and apparel companies. We probably talked with 20 or 30 different companies, just meet-and-greet type conversations. Nothing serious.

We happened to see Tom and Irene Wargo at the PGA Show, though we didn't recognize him until they had already walked by. Then Freddie grabbed my arm and said, "Oh, my gosh, Robert, that was Tom Wargo!" Roland, who was walking along behind us, told us later that people were doing the same kind of thing with Freddie and me all day. "There goes Robert Landers and his wife," they would whisper.

Jerry stayed in Orlando to have more concrete talks with manufacturers, while Freddie, Roland and I headed on to Miami the next day. When we left Azle, Connie Chung's CBS crew had filmed us packing up, leaving the farm, closing the gate and driving past the Azle and Fort Worth city limits signs. Now they wanted to film us arriving in Miami, checking into the hotel, and going to the golf course. It worked out pretty well, though, because, to be honest, we didn't really know where we were going in Miami, and we might have gotten lost otherwise.

I played a practice round on Sunday at the Links at Key Biscayne and shot a 73. The next day was the Monday Pro-Am. It was cold and rainy, and I shot 78, which wasn't all that bad under the conditions. My team finished in fourth place and I won $400. I wrote down the clubs I hit poor shots with, so that during the next session on the range, I could work on them.

In Tuesday's practice round, I shot 70, which was 1-under par. Then in the Wednesday Pro-Am, I shot 78 again. The difference in the scores was mostly putting. I made almost 100 feet of putts on Tuesday and considerably fewer on Monday and Wednesday. That just shows you how important that one little putting statistic is to making a good score.

On Thursday, I played a practice round with Buddy Allin over at the Doral Blue course. I could tell he was going to be one of my better friends. Buddy is really low-key and stays out of sight and away from everything. When I see his left hand, where he's got a callous in his palm the size of a pecan, it's like I haven't practiced at all. I have a lot of respect for that guy. Plus he's nice and treats me really well.

After the Monday Pro-Am, Freddie and I went to the awards dinner that followed. Back in Tampa, when I qualified for the 1995 Senior PGA Tour, Tour officials had a little initiation for the qualifiers, and told us one of the things we were expected to do was to go to at least one Pro-Am dinner every week. But in Miami, Freddie and I noticed that not too many of the Tour players showed up.

One of the things I've figured out is, if it happens that I don't have a pass to play in 1996, that anything I can do right now to improve my chances for getting a sponsor's exemption for next year, is what I'll do. So even though Freddie and I have never been social-type people, or never really felt comfortable in big groups, we'll be right there.

Freddie and I went into this banquet hall, where people were standing around eating and drinking. We soon discovered, to our surprise, that the people at the party were from everywhere, not just Miami. We sat down at a table and pretty soon a couple came over and asked if they could join us.

We figured they were locals, but it turned out they were from Baltimore, Maryland. They were Vicki and John Voit, and they had flown in just so she could play in the Pro-Am. We couldn't quite believe that.

Vicki kept twisting in her seat, and looking around the room. Finally, she said, "I was expecting to see some pros here tonight. I've been looking everywhere, but I haven't seen a single one."

Freddie pointed over at me and said, "Well, he's a pro."

Vicki looked me over. "You're a pro?" she asked. "Who are you?"

I told them, I was Robert Landers from Azle, Texas, and introduced my wife, Freddie. I said that this was our first tournament on the Senior PGA Tour. We got to talking and laughing, and really had a good time. Finally Vicki said, "Oh, Robert, I wish I was playing with you in the Pro-Am tomorrow, but I'm playing with Herb Smith. I don't know who he is."

"Well, I'll introduce you," I said. I led her over to Herb, who I met at qualifying school and who I'd seen standing not far away. I gave them a chance to get acquainted.

Instead of the nice couple from Baltimore, I played in the Pro-Am with four representatives of the Swiss Bank of Key Biscayne, one of the tournament's major sponsors. Our group consisted of bankers from Panama, Guatemala, Argentina and Canada, and me. Fortunately, no one wanted to talk about banking, or international finance, because I wouldn't have had much to say. Instead they wanted to talk about golf, which is something I can do.

On Thursday, the night before the tournament started, I appeared on a live TV show at Don Shula's restaurant. Freddie and I rode down there in a limousine with Butch Davis, the former, Dallas Cowboys, defensive coach, and the new, head coach for the University of Miami Hurricanes. Butch told me that he wanted a picture of me for his office, which made me feel very special.

In the second round on Saturday, I followed my opening 75 with a 79. For the second straight day, I played 18 holes without making a birdie. This is from a guy who begins each round with a goal of making at least three birdies.

Weather conditions were pretty tough. It was windy, I mean really windy. For example, I hit a drive on the 10th hole that started left of the bunker on the left side of the fairway, but, to my horror, flew into the water on the right side. I mean the ball must have moved 100 yards, with a 40-mph wind pushing it from behind. The point being, I'm not sure I could have hit that shot any better, and it still went in the water. It was just one of those days.

In the first round, I had played with Ben Smith, a fellow Texan, whom I had met years ago at a amateur tournament, and Harry Toscano, a real muscular, long-driving guy from Pennsylvania. Ben was an auto mechanic in Grand Prairie before joining the Senior PGA Tour, and Harry operated a driving range in his hometown in Pennsylvania. I guess we were billed as kind of a "blue-collar" threesome, which was fine by me. I was just happy to be out there for my first Tour event.

I was touched when the gallery gave me a big round of applause on the first tee. And, believe it or not, I didn't have much trouble taking the club back for my first shot on Tour. I felt pretty secure, mainly because the fairway had plenty of room to the right—and that's the side where most of my misses go.

In the second round, my playing partners were Bruce Devlin, the veteran Australian, and Bob Reith, who I really wasn't familiar with. They were both nice guys and good players to watch. The highlight of the second round was the appearance of "The Moo Crew." A group of fans showed up wearing these little white-and-black Holstein cow hats, and the media quickly started calling them "The Moo Crew." They started "Mooing" after I hit a shot or made a putt, as a kind of applause.

The first time I heard them, I wasn't sure if they were mooing or booing. My main concern was that the other players weren't going to be put out with me because of what was happening with the gallery. That's really what I was concerned about most—not creating a sideshow that could disturb the other guys.

In the third round at Key Biscayne, I played with Ken Still and Calvin Peete. Calvin's real quiet and goes about his business, but Ken is the kind who enjoys himself on the golf course. He has an outgoing personality and seems to have a lot of fun. He told me right quick that if I had any problems, or needed to talk to anyone about anything, he'd be there for me. I appreciated that.

The good news was I finally broke the birdie drought. It took me until the final nine holes on Sunday, my 48th hole of the tournament, but I finally bagged one. After playing the back nine first, and getting shut out again, I hit a 5-iron to the 184-yard par-3 third hole and sank a 14-footer. Hallelujah!

I told Ken Still before we started the final round that I'd been shut out two straight days. "Don't worry, you'll make a birdie today," he said. "And I want you to remember that I was keeping your score when you made your first one." I reckon that's something I will remember forever.

I had 29 putts in the final round, finally breaking 30 putts for the first time, but I only hit nine greens in regulation and when you do that, you need something like 26 or 27 putts. For the week, I averaged 30.6 putts a round, which is way too many. And I only made one birdie in three rounds, not near my goal of at least nine.

*

A GROUP OF FANS WERE WEARING WHITE AND BLACK HOLSTEIN COW HATS, AND THE MEDIA STARTED CALLING THEM "THE MOO CREW."

The statistics I keep to show me what part of my game needs work made it plain that I didn't have a very good week. I made my chip ups 58 percent of the time, where 80 percent is my goal. I hit 69 percent of the fairways, and I need to hit 80 percent. I made 58.3 feet of putts each round, when my target is 80 feet. My scores of 75-79-74/222 put me in a tie for 62nd place, out of a field of 78 players. For the week I officially earned $1,275, which, for the past few years, is more than Freddie and I brought home in a good month. So it wasn't all bad.

There was one other highlight of our first week on the Senior PGA Tour. We met some people at the Sheraton Biscayne Bay Hotel associated with Travelpro, a company that makes quality luggage. They had seen or read that Freddie and I didn't have any nice luggage, and that we had packed our clothes in trash bags when we went to Tour qualifying school last fall. They offered to give us some.

We said thank you, and that it was very nice, but that they would have to talk to Jerry Hamilton about all that. Jerry worked out a deal, and they met us in the lobby, gave us six pieces of luggage and took a picture of us for their advertising purposes. Jerry told us later, that the luggage retails for about $1,100.

The Travelpro people also wanted to talk to me about some sort of sponsorship. I referred them to Jerry. I've had all kinds of people contact me with all sorts of offers, but I'd rather Jerry sort through these possibilities. He is much more objective about these deals than I would be. I'm the sort who would start feeling more about the person I'm talking to than the offer. Freddie and I are the kind of people who, if someone's nice and sincere and we like them, are tempted to say "yes" to whatever they might be asking. That's the way we are. We trust people to do the things they say they're going to do. That might be naive, but that's how we are.

We enjoyed getting to know Ken Heideger and Bob Cunningham, who are vice-presidents with Travelpro, and Bob's wife, Tanya. Little did we know they had another surprise in store for us.

We had gone out to dinner at Joe's Stone Crab, which I learned is one of the most famous restaurants in all of South

Florida. Personally, Freddie and I don't ever go to restaurants on the weekend, especially on a Friday night. It doesn't make any sense to me to go anywhere where there's a big crowd and too much noise to eat in peace. I avoid that kind of stuff. It's just not us. I know some people consider eating out a social occasion and a good time, but if that's a good time, it's just not for us. We'd rather be at home.

This was a special deal for us though, with a big group of friends from Azle and Fort Worth. The restaurant's management recognized us and gave us a big table, even though there was a long line of people waiting. We ate stone crab, which tasted really good. The bill came to something over a $1,000. Jerry told Jeff Rude, the pro golf writer with *The Dallas Morning News*, "It's a wonderful place for a family of sixteen to eat for under $1,200." I still don't know who paid the bill.

When we got back to our room Saturday night, there was a cocktail napkin from the bar stuck under the door. Someone—the Travelpro people, we later discovered—had written on the napkin "Hope This Helps." Next to it was a yellow piece of paper with some scribbling, that looked to me like Arabic.

Freddie said she was going to find out what it all meant. She called down to the front desk, and the hotel clerk said we had a zero balance on the room.

"Your hotel bill has been taken care of," he told Freddie, who said her jaw dropped. The Travelpro people had paid for everything.

Freddie and I talked that night about how uncomfortable all this attention makes us feel. We're used to working hard and paying our own way. We're not used to having people give us things for free, or pay for our meals or lodging, but both of us slept real well that night, knowing that, for whatever reason, a lot of golf fans out there really do care about us.

I guess our first week on the Senior PGA Tour was a success, even though I'd have liked to have played better. At least I got a tournament under my belt. ESPN had me up in the booth for an interview, even though I wasn't in contention, and I got to show off my Dickies cap and my Cross Timbers sweater.

Cross Timbers is a public course in Azle that opened for play in February 1995. It's a project I've been helping the city with for several years, a dream come true for golfers in my hometown. Cross Timbers was a goal of mine long before I even started to think about attempting professional golf.

All the Senior PGA Tour players have been receptive to me and extremely supportive. It seems like the opinions I hear, and I don't know anybody who's said any different, is that my presence will be good for the Senior PGA Tour.

I hope so, because that's the way I want it to be. If I thought my being here was anything different from that, I'd be trying to make some changes, either in myself or with the people around me.

I'm not coming out on the Senior PGA Tour with a selfish attitude. That's just not the way I am. I want to be good for the game of golf, and I want to do anything I can to help the Tour, to help the tournament sponsors and to make a contribution.

People ask me all the time about my goals for the 1995 Senior PGA Tour. Is it to win a tournament? Is it to compete against legends of golf like Arnold Palmer, Jack Nicklaus, Gary Player, Lee Trevino and Raymond Floyd?

I've repeatedly said my only goal is to do well enough to earn an exemption for 1996, by finishing in the top 31 Tour money winners this year. If I work hard and have patience, I think I'll have my chance. I'm certainly going to try my hardest to succeed.

Mainly, though, Freddie and I are out here to make the most of this once-in-a-lifetime opportunity. We want to enjoy this impossible dream come true.

Chapter Two

WHEN YOU'RE HOT, YOU'RE HOT

Ever since November 1994, when I earned playing privileges for the 1995 Senior PGA Tour, the predictable, routine part of our lives has become history. My finish at the Senior PGA Tour National Qualifying Tournament earned me one of eight full exemptions, making me eligible to compete in all the 1995 Senior PGA Tour's open, co-sponsored tournaments. That includes almost every event, except the Tournament of Champions, the PGA Seniors' Championship, the Senior U.S. Open and maybe one or two others.

As it stands, I should be able to play in about 33 Senior PGA Tour tournaments in 1995. If I stay healthy, I intend to be there for all of them.

I shot qualifying rounds of 72-72-71-73 for 288, four over par, at the TPC of Tampa Bay, a pretty tough course with plenty of water. Fortunately, I kept my ball more or less dry during the four rounds, losing only two balls in the drink in four days (I fished a couple balls out with my ball retriever; I also noticed I was the only player there carrying one). A lot of fellows weren't quite as lucky in avoiding the water. My final score tied me for sixth place with Bobby Mitchell, 10 strokes behind the low qualifier, Tommy Aycock.

I earned $4,270 for the week. That may not sound like much, compared with today's big purses in professional golf, but for a fellow who had been out of work for a couple of years, trying to make ends meet by selling firewood in the winter and second-hand stuff at flea markets in the summer, it was a huge payday. I'd never made that much money in one week in my entire life. Not at Mitchell's Department Store, where I worked for 20 years before the company shut the store which I managed in Azle, and certainly not as a jet engine mechanic in the United States Air Force. Or any of the other jobs I had after leaving Texas Christian University, where I was a music education major.

I'D NEVER MADE THAT MUCH MONEY IN ONE WEEK IN MY ENTIRE LIFE.

To be honest, I really couldn't believe what transpired in Tampa. If anyone had asked me what my chances were to earn a tour card as a 51-year-old nobody from nowhere, I'd have said probably a million to one. Maybe higher. Many of the guys in the 111-player field at Tampa had years of experience on the PGA Tour and some of them, like Buddy Allin, Gary Groh, and Bobby Mitchell had won PGA Tour events. More than a few had played on the 1994 Senior PGA Tour, meaning they were tournament-tested and had the competitive edge golf generally requires.

Other than playing two rounds in the 1980 U.S. Open at Baltusrol, where I missed the cut, the closest I'd ever come to a really big-time professional golf event was going over to Colonial Country Club in Fort Worth to watch the pros in the Colonial National Invitation. It turned out to be something I didn't especially enjoy, because I quickly found out that I'd much rather play golf myself than stand around watching someone else play, even if that someone happens to be Jack Nicklaus, Lee Trevino, Tom Watson, Ray Floyd or any of the world's best players.

I don't enjoy watching golf tournaments on TV, either. They make me too nervous. Freddie will watch them, but when they come on, I usually go out and hit balls in our two-acre front yard.

The biggest listing on my golf resume before Tampa was three-time winner of the Fort Worth City Amateur Championship, which I knew wouldn't strike any fear into the hearts of my fellow competitors. I wasn't exactly tournament tough, either. Other than the Senior PGA Tour Regional Qualifying one week earlier at Woodlake Country Club in San Antonio, where I finished ninth and earned my ticket to Tampa, I'd played in exactly two tournaments in 1994— the Texas State Open in August and the Texoma Senior Open in Lawton, Oklahoma, in October. If this had been a thoroughbred race, the notation next to my name in the racing form would probably have read something like "lightly tested."

One thing that helped me earn my card in Tampa (actually, the TPC of Tampa Bay course is in Lutz, one of the suburbs) was the blustery weather conditions. High winds, generated by tropical storm Gordon, were giving everybody fits, but because I basically hit a low ball, my shots weren't being buffeted as much as some of the others.

My opening round of 72, on a day when the winds were gusting to 40 mph, was good for a tie for fourth. That seemed to take off some of the pressure, because guys who shot in the high 70s, or low 80s, suddenly were forced to try and play catch up. TPC-Tampa Bay is not the kind of course where you can make a lot of birdies, so I tried to stick to my game plan, shooting to the middle of the greens, trying to avoid the water and doing my best to hang somewhere around par. It worked.

The hallmark of my game has always been steadiness. That's the way I taught myself to play golf, taking the time to figure out where the real trouble was on a golf course, and how I could avoid it. I always made managing my misses the first priority.

A lot of people don't have the patience to play golf that way. They'd rather hit a few spectacular shots than a whole lot of safe, unspectacular ones. My method has always been to take a conservative, low-risk approach to golf, and it's served me reasonably well. Never better than my memorable week in Florida.

When I came off the 18th green after the final round at Tampa Bay, I had tears in my eyes. So did Freddie. I gave her a big kiss and wrapped her up in a big hug. It's hard to say which one of us was doing more crying, shaking and trembling. It might have been a tie. I signed my scorecard after my playing partner, Bob E. Smith, who also finished in the top eight, helped me go over all the numbers slowly and carefully.

I'd played nine holes with Bob E. Smith the day before the tournament began. It was a miserable day. The wind was howling, and after we finished the front side, he said he'd had enough. He said the wind wasn't doing his game any good. After watching me hit my low shots underneath the gusts, he made a prediction. "Robert," he said, "you're going to be the big story this week. You're going to get your Tour card."

The magnitude of my accomplishment suddenly began to sink in, as I realized I was going to the 1995 Senior PGA Tour. "This is amazing," I told a sports writer with one of the Tampa newspapers. "This is my lifelong dream come true. The impossible dream."

"We poor-manned it all the way," Freddie told the same reporter. "Nobody thought we could do it. Everybody said golf is too expensive. It's not the way we do it."

We headed back to Texas the next day, driving straight through for 20 hours. We were too excited to stop, other than for gas and food. We splurged on one meal, stopping at a Waffle House instead of our usual, McDonald's. Freddie made a fuss when I left the waitress a $2 tip, but what the heck, for once I had money in my pocket. We were giddy, either laughing or crying, the entire trip.

One of the reasons we had to get home in a hurry was because I had promised to deliver to several folks some firewood by Thanksgiving. One lady wanted me to cut some wood 15" in length, which is little-bitty and takes some extra-fine work, and I'd told her I'd take care of her. A man's only as good as his word, so whenever I tell someone I'll do something, I do my best to get the job done.

I delivered the lady a half-cord of 15" wood and stacked it on her porch. Without any other discussion, she handed me a check for $120. I said, "Hold on, ma'am. That's too much money. That's for a whole cord, and all I could bring you was a half-cord worth $65."

"I thought it was going to be $120," she said.

"No ma'am," I said. "If anyone tries to sell you this much wood for $120 and tells you it's a cord, they're wrong. I told her to write me out another check, because I wasn't about to take advantage of her.

It's funny, but before we went to Tampa, Freddie always nagged me to stop hitting so many golf balls and to cut more firewood. But as soon as I qualified for the Senior PGA Tour, she told me to stop cutting so much wood and start hitting more golf balls.

When we sat down for Thanksgiving dinner, we commented about just how much we had to be thankful for. We realized we have been blessed beyond our wildest imagination. Freddie and I would have been happy to live the rest of our lives on the farm, contented as Elsie the Cow, but a whole new world had suddenly opened up for us. We could definitely see greener pastures ahead.

Almost immediately after Tampa, the press picked up on the story of the golfing farmer, who had come out of a cow pasture in Texas and qualified for the Senior PGA Tour. Writers referred to me as a "Cinderella" story and the "Rocky" of golf. A writer from *Sports Illustrated* named Franz Lidz flew down to Texas right after Thanksgiving and visited the farm. He did a nice write up, and they took pictures of me hitting balls with the cows milling around. The photographer even had me and Freddie pose for a picture like the famous Grant Wood painting called "American Gothic," only I was holding a handful of irons instead of a pitchfork.

Not long after that, we had a visit from a TV crew from CNN News. Then the people with Connie Chung's CBS show, "Eye To Eye," came and camped out in Azle. It got so that our farm was turning into such a media circus that my little pooch, Oleo, was running her legs off racing back and forth to the front gate to greet all our guests. No telling what the cows thought about all this commotion.

I even got a call at home one day from Lee Trevino, extending me a welcome to the Senior PGA Tour. "Whatever happens, Robert," Trevino told me, "don't change anything you've done to get here. And take advantage of the opportunity you have. Play as much golf as you possibly can. Just be sure to get plenty of rest." Which was some really good advice that I planned to follow. Chi Chi Rodriguez also wrote a short personal note, offering his congratulations. Chi Chi's been a big booster of mine right from the start.

Soon after the avalanche of publicity began, Freddie and I started getting mail from people all over the country. John Hall and Mike Hall of Hall Lumber Sales in Middleton, Wisconsin sent us two checks for $400. They and some of their friends had pooled some money to help us cover expenses on the Senior PGA Tour. John Hall extended his best wishes and added a postscript to his letter that read: "P.S. If you are successful, please help some other deserving person."

This is something I intend to do. I'm making plans to set up a scholarship fund through the Sertoma Club in Azle to help some young golfers in our area—Azle, Springtown or somewhere close— with money for college. I intend to put in as much money for the kids as all these strangers have sent to us.

Other folks sent us $5 or $10, sometimes with a check, sometimes in cash. We received some letters of congratulations simply addressed to "Robert Landers c/o Azle, Texas" on the front of the envelope. One letter had been sent directly to *Golf World* in Connecticut, which had done a story on my surprising success, and it was forwarded to the farm. I'm glad our local postmaster knew where to find us.

All the money came in pretty handy, because by the middle of December, our bank account was getting pretty skinny. My winnings from Tampa didn't arrive until around Christmas. What extra money we had on hand, we put into buying more cedar stays for our fence, which had fallen into disrepair, since Freddie and I had lost our jobs, but we sure couldn't afford to have any cattle wandering off.

We also received monetary support from folks in the immediate area who were eager to help us out. My friends Steve Champion, Steve Henton and Jim Laird got together and organized a benefit golf tournament at Squaw Creek in Willow Springs.

Steve Champion happens to be the golf professional at Casino Beach Golf Academy, a driving range and executive course in Lake Worth, where I've practiced a good bit in recent years. Jim Laird, who owns Laird Technical Distribution in Azle, is a fellow I got involved in golf last summer. I gave him his first lesson in chipping and pitching out in the pasture at the farm.

Steve Henton, a former golf professional, is now the minister at Rockwood Christian Church in Fort Worth. Steve performed a private ceremony at his house on March 9, 1990, when Freddie and I exchanged wedding vows. Steve said before the service that I shouldn't worry about having to pay him anything, but in case I had recently won any golf balls as prizes, he could sure use a few, so I gave him a dozen new golf balls.

* I SURE DON'T FIT THE MOLD OF YOUR TYPICAL SCRATCH GOLFER. NEVER HAVE, NEVER WILL.

Steve Henton once told me that when he first started his job as an assistant golf professional at Pecan Valley in Fort Worth, one of his associates in the pro shop pointed me out as I was standing on the practice green. "Hey, Steve," the guy said, "see that fellow over there in the cowboy shirt, blue jeans and tennis shoes?"

"Yeah," said Steve. "What about him?"

"That's Robert Landers. He can beat anyone in Fort Worth."

"Him?" said Steve, unimpressed with the golfing specimen he was looking at. "You've got to be kidding me. He looks like a complete hacker." Which is the honest-to-goodness truth. I do look like your average 20-handicapper, even when I assume my stance, take my grip and start my backswing, which goes about two-thirds of the way back and makes Doug Sanders or Dan Pohl look like they take a big rip. It's not until I make contact with the ball that anyone would suspect anything different.

I sure don't fit the mold of your typical scratch golfer. Never have, never will. With my homemade swing and hand-me-down golf attire, I look more like a plowman than a player. So I can understand how Steve might have been fooled by my appearance. A lot of people have been.

The benefit tournament wasn't something I necessarily wanted them to do, but since they're my good friends, and they seemed really keen on the idea, I finally said okay. They held the tournament on Monday, December 12, and something like 100 people, who paid $50 each, showed up, and not just Azle and Fort Worth folks, either. People came up from Austin and down from Oklahoma, and one couple showed up from Iowa. The tournament raised about $2,600, after expenses and the guys turned the proceeds over to us. Danny Vasquez, who won $35 in a putting contest at the tournament, gave us that money, too.

About the same time, Steve Champion got a call from a fellow in Savannah, Tennessee, named Danny Wells, who wanted to do something to help. Turns out Danny had played sports at Brewer H.S. in White Settlement at the same time I was playing football at Azle High. We even knew some of the same people, though not each other. Steve talked to Danny about how to organize a benefit golf tournament in Savannah, and his event raised another $1,300.

To be honest, Freddie and I felt a bit overwhelmed by all the support we were receiving from people we'd never met. I guess it goes to show there's a lot of well-intentioned folks in this world, people with good hearts who genuinely care about others.

With all the stories circulating about this upstart from Azle, Texas—Jeff Rude, the Dallas, golf writer, referred to me as the "wonder farmer"—golf fans seemed fascinated most by the fact that I play golf in tennis shoes, and that I use homemade clubs.

Those are two easy topics to explain. First, I wear tennis shoes (size 10 or $10^{1}/_{2}$, depending on the brand) when I play golf primarily because they're comfortable. Beyond that, I've spent hundreds of hours hitting golf balls in sneakers, so I figure I might as well go ahead and play in them. In fact, I'd recommend that more golfers practice, or play, in tennis shoes, because they help you learn to keep your balance. If you get off-balance swinging in sneakers, you'll slide all over the place and never make solid contact with the ball.

Finally, tennis shoes don't leave any spike marks on the greens, and as we all know, there are few things more likely to ruin a fun round of golf than spiked up greens. Especially after you've hit your approach shot close to the pin and have a short birdie putt, only to get to the green and find that you have to negotiate a bunch of mini-speed bumps. Bumps left behind by some golfer's big feet.

Freddie bought me a new pair of Foot-Joy golf shoes to wear at Tampa, but I decided to stick with my trusty Reeboks and L.A. Gear sneakers because I was afraid I might drag my heels and scuff up the greens. Freddie was concerned that I'd look like a hick from the sticks playing in tennis shoes, but I told her not to mind. They don't give you style points in golf for your attire—or your shoes.

They don't give you style points for having a pretty swing, either, which is something else I don't have. All they do in golf is add up all the strokes and see who's the lowest, or, as was the case in Tampa, those who are the lowest 16 (besides the eight players that received full exemptions, guys who finished in the 9th through 16th spots gained conditional playing privileges).

Freddie was concerned that people in Tampa might make fun of us for looking like poor people. Personally, I don't care one way or the other about such things. I'm as comfortable wearing $1 golf shirts that I've bought at flea markets or garage sales as I would be if I bought a $20 golf shirt in a store. Some of the golf pants in my closet cost maybe $2, tops. If they're clean—and they fit—who cares how much you paid for them?

I'm more interested in what a person is really like than what he or she looks like. I'm more interested in what they're made of, if they have a good heart, than what they're wearing on their backs. I'm just not clothes-conscious at all, which might seem a bit strange, since I spent 20 years working for a clothing store.

As far as using homemade golf clubs, well, when you don't have a lot of extra money, it's pretty hard to justify buying a full set of Pings or Cobras or Calloways or Wilsons—or any of those top-line equipment brands. In 1989, some years after I started building and repairing golf clubs, I had put together a set of component irons for my cousin, Steven Sosebee. After awhile, he said he was tired of them and wanted to change clubs, so I bought the set back from him for $70.

When I qualified at Tampa, I also had a $20 golf bag I'd bought from Steve Henton, a Hulk three-wood I bought for $12 (I put in a graphite shaft that I'd found in a garbage can), an $18 putter I got from the Golfsmith catalog and my one extravagance, a $58 Big Brother driver with a boron graphite shaft. So I had a total of $158 invested in the clubs—$178, if you count the bag.

Like the cost of attire, price isn't the issue in golf equipment, accuracy is. I mean, which would you rather have in your bag: a $1,000 customized set of clubs that you can't hit a lick with, or a $100 set of clubs that you can flat nail on the screws? That's easy.

It's not hard to figure out, either, why I seldom wear a golf glove when I play. At first it was because I never had an extra $8 or $10 to spend on one. For years, my first wife, Barbara, kept me on a strict allowance of $20 a week, and I tried hard to conserve that money so I could get in one round of golf on the weekend. Besides, golf gloves, sooner or later wear out. Your hands won't wear out. They'll just get tougher and coarser, and you'll develop bigger callouses.

Our phone had been ringing off the wall ever since Tampa, and one day in December, I got a call from some fellow in Hollywood. The conversation was real general and preliminary, but the caller said he wanted to make a biographical movie about my life. He said the film had the potential to be another "Rudy," the inspirational story of the football player who walked-on at Notre Dame, or another "Rocky" or "Field of Dreams." I can't remember if he said anything about "Forrest Gump," but he might have. He was talking pretty fast.

When I told Freddie about the phone call from Hollywood, she immediately sounded like a casting director.

"If they make a movie about our lives, I hope Jaclyn Smith plays me," she said.

When I heard her say that, I piped up: "Well, if Jaclyn Smith plays you, then I want to play myself."

Most of the phone calls we were receiving came from golf club and golf ball manufacturers. Strangers were calling me up at all hours of the day and night, offering me all kinds of money to endorse their clubs or their balls. When you're hot, you're hot.

I knew right away I would need some help sorting out all the offers. So in early December, I went over to Dallas and met with a couple of player representatives, including Rocky Hambric of Cornerstone Sports, who handles many of the top players on the PGA Tour, like Corey Pavin, Phil Mickelson and Mark Brooks, who grew up playing at Diamond Oaks in Fort Worth. I called Mark to ask him a few questions, and he gave Cornerstone Sports, and his personal manager, David Winkle, a real solid recommendation. I also met with David Parker of Links MMG, who handles several senior players, among them Jim Albus. David's an old friend from Fort Worth, who I first met when he was an assistant pro at Ridglea Country Club.

There was no doubt that either Cornerstone Sports or Links MMG could have helped me get some endorsements right away. But before I went to Dallas to meet with those people, my step-mother, Evelyn Landers, passed away.

Evelyn had been suffering from Alzheimer's Disease for some time. All her medical care had put my dad under a lot of stress, as well as something of a financial burden. I was prepared to sign right away with one of the Dallas companies, hoping that they would line up some endorsement deals quickly. I really wanted to help my dad meet some of the expenses associated with Evelyn's care. With her passing, though, the need for immediate action on my part was removed.

After the Dallas meetings, I had time to think things over for a few days and discuss all the options with Freddie. I finally decided to let Jerry Hamilton serve as my business manager and agent. Jerry's an old friend, who I first met when he was a freelance sports writer working for several area newspapers, including the local weekly, the *Azle News*. Jerry came by my office at Mitchell's Department Store one day to do a story about a charity golf event I was running through the Sertoma Club.

We struck up a friendship, and later began playing golf together at courses like Z. Boaz in Fort Worth, Live Oak in Weatherford, Squaw Creek in Willow Springs, Sugar Tree in Dennis and over at his home course, Holiday Hills, in Mineral Wells. A real outgoing guy, Jerry's also been a golf pro and has run his family's tire store in Mineral Wells. He's also put on a number of local golf tournaments, so I figured, with all his contacts and savvy, he could represent my interests well. I gave him the job, and he got a friend of his from Mineral Wells, an attorney named George Gault, to act as my legal counsel.

As I mentioned, I also told Roland Sparks he could work as my caddie when we went out on Tour. Roland and I have played a lot of golf together, and he probably knows my game as well as anyone. I'll never forget the first time we played together, in a partnership tournament down at P.A.R. Country Club in Comanche, Texas.

Roland's sister-in-law, Geneva Pruitt, who worked at Mitchell's from the time the store opened in Azle in 1967 until it closed in 1992, and who is, without a doubt, the best cook who ever lived, was always telling him that I was a pretty decent golfer. I'm not sure Roland believed her, so he took me with him to a partnership tournament in Comanche to check me out. It was a three-day deal, and neither one of us did much good the first two days. But on the back nine of the third round, I caught fire. I made seven birdies and shot 29. I guess I made a believer out of ol' Roland right then and there. The way I played that day was almost as fine as Geneva Pruitt's famous banana pudding. But not quite.

BUT ON THE BACK NINE OF THE THIRD ROUND, I CAUGHT FIRE. I MADE SEVEN BIRDIES AND SHOT 29.

Anyway, Freddie and I spent the rest of December 1994 making plans for going out on the 1995 Senior PGA Tour. We worked it out so that Freddie's daughters, Vicky Hall and Lisa Rose, would look in on the farm and keep the cattle fed. Lonnie Corley, my lifelong friend, would keep an eye on the place, too.

One of the nicest things about living in the country is that neighbors will pitch in and help each other. We're all pretty independent and self-sufficient people, but when someone has a need, country folks are always there for each other. You can count on it.

Freddie was getting concerned about how we would be accepted out on tour, how we would fit in. She said she was afraid we might stick out like a couple of sore thumbs. I told her, "We are who we are, so what's the point of trying to be anything different? We have to be ourselves." I don't know if that made her feel any better or not, but I figured we had better things to worry about than that.

Right before Christmas, I made my first live guest-appearance on television—the "Good Morning Texas" program on WFAA-TV in Dallas. Freddie was excited because one of the co-hosts, Scott Sams, used to be weatherman on Channel 8 and has always been one of her favorite TV people. Jerry was excited because his nephew, Sean Hamilton, is one of the assistant producers of the show. I got excited, too, especially when Jerry told me that I had to put on makeup to do the interview. I thought he was joking at first, but before I went out there in front of the cameras, I had to get my cheeks and forehead powdered.

Talking with Scott and his co-host, Deborah Duncan, was the easy part of the interview. The hard part when I was asked to putt, live and in living color. This was made even more difficult when Deborah and Scott each took a shot and sank their putts, right before I took my turn on the 10 foot carpet runner. Talk about pressure: I had to make the putt or look pretty foolish.

Fortunately, I clutch-stabbed it into the hole. The funny thing was, though, that I had been practicing that putt for about 10 or 15 minutes before we went on the air, and I never made it. Not once!

By early January 1995, Jerry brought us an endorsement offer from Dickies. Dickies, which has its headquarters in Fort Worth, manufactures work clothes. Dickies is a brand we used to sell at Mitchell's Department Store, and I felt honored to have the chance to represent such a fine company. I've had experience with Dickies ever since 1960, when, as an 11th grader, I got my first job as a stock boy at the Mitchell's Department Store in Lake Worth.

The way the deal came about, I guess, is that after Mike Capps, who's with CNN News, did the TV piece, he went home and told his wife, Dee, who handles advertising for Dickies, about us. Next thing I knew, Dee was calling us, expressing an interest in a sponsorship. For several years, Dickies had been sponsoring Walt Zembriski, a former ironworker and the mini-tour player, who's had such a great career on the Senior PGA Tour. Now they also had an interest in me.

Jerry, Steve Champion and I went over to talk with Dee and Jim McLaughlin, another Dickies executive. The conversation was real friendly and pretty low-key, and they came up with an offer we couldn't refuse and gratefully accepted.

Under the terms of the arrangement, I will wear a Dickies cap on the Senior PGA Tour throughout 1995. I'll also do some promotional work for the company, like conducting a few golf outings with some of their customers and prospects. Dickies also plans to use me in some of its advertising, like the ad that has been running in *Parade* for a couple of months now.

In return, Dickies agreed to pay us $47,000, which pretty well blew us away. At the rate things were going before I made the Senior PGA Tour, that amount was more than four years' wages for Freddie and me. See what I mean about greener pastures?

The other neat thing about the Dickies' deal—which we agreed to on my 51st birthday (January 6) and was the biggest birthday gift I'll ever receive—is that they invited us to go by the outlet store near downtown Fort Worth and pick up a few things. We got a bunch of hats, jeans and T-shirts for ourselves and our family members, and I picked up a few Dickies T-shirts for Roland to wear while he caddies on the Senior PGA Tour.

Maybe the best thing, though, was that I got a bunch of Dickies work gloves. They're much better than the gloves I'd been buying at local flea markets. While splitting wood and working with fences and barbed wire, I'd go through a pair of those cheap gloves every week. The Dickies gloves would last.

Freddie and I celebrated my birthday, and our new Dickies deal, by going to out to dinner at the Mesquite Pit in Weatherford. We were joined by Jerry and Kathy Hamilton, and another couple from Mineral Wells, Charles and Dollie Gatlin. Freddie insisted on paying for dinner, and she did, but when she saw that the bill was over $80, she took a deep breath and swallowed hard. I haven't seen her reaching for any tabs since—certainly not the one at Joe's Stone Crab down in Florida.

We also got a call from a real estate man in California named Tim Hoctor, who said he was so moved by the story he read about us in *Sports Illustrated* that he wanted to put us up at his house during the week in February, when the tour was in Ojai for the FHP Health Care Classic. He also said he'd loan us his pick-up truck, a classic '64 Chevy. Freddie and I talked the idea over and decided we wouldn't feel comfortable staying in anyone's home, so we declined the invitation.

Then Tim sent us a letter, including pictures of him, his neighbor, and the Ojai course. Later, he called back and said he had a friend named Matt Ellison, who was volunteering to pay for our week at a luxury inn near Ojai. All we had to do was come out to California a day early and play a round of golf with Tim and Matt. So we said, "Sure, let's do it."

A few weeks later, Tim called back to tell us that Matt had been playing golf in a pro-am and made a hole-in-one, winning a new $50,000 BMW. When Jerry Hamilton heard that, he said, "Robert, good luck seems to rub off on everybody you run into. Here's five dollars. Would you mind stopping at Dollar Bill's and buying me some Texas lottery tickets?"

As January raced by, we got ready to go on tour. Freddie went to Fort Worth and bought a few new outfits to wear. Jerry started talking to the people at LaMode about getting me some golf clothes, and to the people at Titleist about having me play their ball. Incidentally, I like playing with balls that have high numbers on them, like Titleist 5s, for example, because I always try to beat the number on the ball.

Meanwhile, we kept hearing from all kinds of equipment manufacturers wanting me to try their golf clubs. When I wasn't giving interviews, which seemed like every other day, I stayed busy hitting shag balls around the farm. At night, after dinner, I spent hours practicing my putting.

Also in January, a few weeks before we headed out on our big adventure, Freddie started letting me putt indoors on the carpet. That was a real breakthrough in my golf career, because previously she'd never let me bring any of my golf stuff inside the house.

There was one thing I knew for sure: If the Senior PGA Tour ever stops at a course where the speed of the greens is about the same as a slow shag carpet, I'll be set to make a killing.

Chapter Three

TAKE YOUR
BEST SHOT

Freddie and I had no way of knowing that 1994 would turn out to be the best year of our lives—or maybe I should say the best year yet. It sure didn't start out that way, though.

Freddie's mother, Winifred Nell Barksdale, became seriously ill on Christmas Day in 1993. We tried calling her all day but never got an answer. It turned out that Freddie's sister, Virginia Dodson, had taken Winifred to the hospital in Killeen, Texas, and the doctors diagnosed her with an acute intestinal blockage. Freddie packed up, left the farm and spent most of the next month down there, looking after her mother.

We were all hoping she was going to get better and be able to come home. Doctors performed surgery, but Winifred never could rally after the operation and slowly started slipping away. She died on January 20, 1994, the day before her 75th birthday. She was buried there in Killeen.

Winifred's serious condition started the year off on a real sour note. We didn't have much enthusiasm for celebrating New Year's Eve, New Year's Day or, for that matter, my 50th birthday on January 6. We were just feeling too low.

On Winifred's birthday in 1993, we had named a new calf "Winnie" in her honor. Winifred was thrilled to death, because she'd never had anything named after her. Shortly after Winifred died, our big, white, Brahma Charolais cow, named Queenie, gave birth to a heifer calf. Freddie insisted that we call the calf Little Gloria, because Winifred believed in angels and Gloria was the name of one of her special ones.

Several days later, I went into the pasture and found Little Gloria lying on her side. Her eyes were open, but they weren't moving. She was dead. Naturally, that sent Freddie into a tailspin. I certainly didn't feel too hot about it, either.

A month or so later, in March 1994, we took several heifers up to my dad's property in Poolville and somehow or other Winnie got loose. She jumped a fence and headed west. We spent a month looking everywhere for her, roaming around the countryside, asking all the neighbors to be on the look out, even contacting the Parker County sheriff's department. But none of it did any good.

We finally gave up our search. Winnie had vanished.

Freddie and I never considered ourselves to be lucky people, but now we were beginning to wonder whether there was a dark cloud hanging over us. I had lost my job at Mitchell's in September 1992, when the store finally closed, and Freddie had lost her job at Medical Designs in Azle, where she made orthopedic shoes, in late 1993.

We were trying as best we could to scratch out a living farming, cutting wood, repairing golf clubs and making cow artifacts—decorative cutouts and knickknacks of Holstein cattle. We even painted cows on old bowling pins and tried to sell them at flea markets. We were keeping our heads above water, but just barely.

About the only positive note in our lives was that by turning 50 in January, I had reached the minimum age to become a senior golfer. I had been thinking about playing in a number of amateur tournaments for seniors, like the Fort Worth City Senior Championship, the Texas Senior Amateur, or maybe even, the U.S. Senior Open. Freddie balked when she heard the idea.

"Robert, if you're going continue to play golf, you'll do so as a professional," she said. "We can't afford to support any amateur golf. And besides, we need the money."

Freddie had a good point, as usual, with both of us being out of work. At 50, I was old enough to play on the Senior PGA Tour. All we needed now was some miracle to make me eligible.

There's probably a thousand or more really good golfers in the United States, professionals and amateurs alike, who are in their late 40s and just marking time until they reach 50 and can take a shot at the Senior PGA Tour, like Benny Passons, who's a club pro and a heckuva player.

Who can blame them? There's so much money to be made in professional golf these days. They don't have cuts in Senior PGA Tour events, which means that even when you're off your game and have a bad week, you'll earn a paycheck of almost $1,000. I can't imagine any deal much better than that, unless it's having a real good week and winning $100,000 of course.

One of the major roadblocks to my career in golf had always been money. I never had income to cover all the expenses associated with playing tournament golf. Friends often asked me why I didn't play in some of the mini-tour events in Texas, like the Lone Star Tour or the Ninfa's Tour (which later combined to form one Texas mini-tour). The reason was the weekly entry fee was something like four or five hundred dollars—money I didn't have to spare.

*

"ROBERT, IF YOU'RE GOING TO CONTINUE TO PLAY GOLF, YOU'LL DO SO AS A PROFES- SIONAL."

So I came up with a plan. I asked my uncle, Tom McDaniel, who's the writer in our family and who's even written a genealogical book on the family's roots, to help me put together a letter that I could send to friends and acquaintances, some of them local businessmen around Azle and Fort Worth, who knew me and my background in golf. My idea was that I'd sell shares in myself and pay the investors back with earnings.

Here's the letter we composed:

Dear...,
As most of my friends know, for a long time I have had a desire to play golf professionally. I have worked hard to perfect my golf game to the

point that I now know I have a chance to play in some tournaments and win some money.

Through the years, whether we have played a lot of golf together or not, I have tried to be one of the top amateurs in the North Texas area. Since I turned fifty a few months ago, the Senior PGA Tour seems to be the answer to the goal that I have had for a long time. I would like you to be a part of it with me. I believe that you will agree that if I am ever going to do it, this year is the time.

Unequivocally, I will need some financial assistance, so I am going to ask ten or twelve of my friends and associates to see if this is possible.

In 1994 help is needed for entry fees and travel expenses. I don't want to play every week and travel a lot, but I do need help with entry fees, and mileage to and from events. The ultimate goal is the Senior PGA Tour Qualifying School.

My proposal to you as a participant in this venture would be a 50/50 split of winnings. There will be winnings! I will work hard!

If there is one or two who wants to form one workable plan or a dozen, please call me and let's get together and talk and see what kind of a business arrangement we can make that will be collectively profitable.

Sincerely,

Robert W. Landers
5540 Sabathney Road
Weatherford, TX 76086
RWL:tm

Uncle Tom and I later composed another letter, which explained in some detail how my plan would work. That letter read:

Dear ...,
After much thought, I am going to divide the 50% into twenty shares (parts). Each investor will be asked to contribute $100.00 for one share. There will be no limit to how many shares each investor can have. When

I have all twenty shares sold, I will not seek additional backers, or share holders.

The reason for twenty shares will be to ensure that there will be enough money available to proceed through a successful project.

The maximum investment for the project is $1,000.00 per share. The time frame for the project will be eighteen months to end approximately November 1995 or the last tournament in which I compete in that month. Depending on our success we will decide at that time whether or not to continue to pursue professional golf.

Tour qualifying could cause additional funds to be needed at one time only (possibly during a two year period). I want to have an opportunity to qualify the second time, which means a second year. Income from the tournaments could suffice, but I want you to know all the facts as I see them. I still do not believe it will run over the $1,000.00 limit.

I appreciate your confidence and trust that we can make this work beneficially for all.

Yours very cordially,

R.W. Landers
RWL:tm

Before I got around to sending out any letters, though, I bounced the first letter off of Freddie to get her reaction. She had an immediate one, all right. Boy, did she ever.

"Robert, if you're going to try to play professional golf you've got to do so on your own," Freddie told me in no uncertain terms. "You have to believe in yourself enough not to go asking other people for their money. Everything you ever got in golf you earned on your own. Why start looking now for outside help? Just get out there and take your best shot."

Freddie had a point. I agreed with her that I should be able to stand, or fall, on my own. So I ditched the idea of sending out a letter asking for money from investors and decided to pay my own way. To do that, I dipped into my life savings.

That amounted to about $9,800, which I had put into an individual retirement account (IRA) during my years with Mitchell's. I never really considered that IRA to be my money—I thought it was ours—Freddie's and mine. I always planned to use the money for family things, having no intention or desire to spend it on myself.

Freddie encouraged me to use that IRA to take my shot at professional golf, and, with her blessing, that's exactly what I did. She made it clear, however, that when the golf money ran out, I would have to go out and find a regular job. Firewood sales and odd-jobs weren't cutting it.

So I surrendered my amateur status and declared myself a professional in April 1994. I made a $1,000 withdrawal from my IRA, which I kept at the Azle State Bank, to cover some expenses and to pay for my entry in the Texas State Open, which was to be played at The Woodlands in Houston in August. It cost $100 for the qualifier at Fossil Creek, where I shot 72 and advanced, and $150 for the tournament.

The Texas State Open is one of my favorite tournaments, because it was the first pro-type event I played in, way back in 1976. I always enjoyed meeting pros from around Texas and comparing my game with theirs. My goals as a amateur were to make the cut in the Texas State Open and to become known as a respectable competitor. I wanted to be able to walk into a pro shop and have the pro recognize me as a real player, and to have some kind of mutual respect between us.

My first tournament as a professional had a reasonably good beginning and a not-so-splendid finish. I shot 74-71 in the first two rounds for 145, which was the cut number when the field was reduced from 240 players to 70. In the final two rounds, I ballooned to 75 and 82, finishing last in the money.

Still, I earned $275 for making the cut—a $25 profit over what it cost me to enter. The one thing I learned at The Woodlands was just how far these young kids are hitting their golf balls these days. Whether it's because of juiced-up balls, high-tech shafts, the flexibility of young muscles—or a combination of all three—it's amazing how far some guys can drive the ball. Their length off the tee, and through the green, makes courses play much shorter and leads to lower scores. The winner, incidentally, was Jeff Maggart, who's one of the best players on the PGA Tour. He shot four straight 68s and blew everyone away.

Up to the very minute I turned professional, I had carefully guarded my amateur status. Believe it or not, some guys have been known to fudge. I have met some good players who were fence-walkers, who would try to make a dollar here or there if they could.

You could always turn pro, simply by declaring yourself to be a professional or writing down "Pro" on an entry form or by accepting prize money. In my opinion, if you win money in a Calcutta pool at your club or muny, you've technically become a professional.

The real deal, in my opinion, was keeping a clean slate and not ever straddling the line. I was proud of my amateur standing and did my best to preserve its integrity—which meant never accepting money or doing anything to jeopardize my status. After I turned pro, that was that.

As the summer of 1994 went along, I stepped up my practice routine in anticipation of upcoming tournaments. I would help Freddie with farm chores each morning, but after lunch I would head out to our pasture and spend the rest of the day hitting golf balls. I probably hit about 300 to 400 balls a day, on average. I was able to work on my long game and short game, everything but putting and sand shots.

We had built a bunker, hauling up sand from the creek bed. Freddie helped me shovel the sand, which I carried up to the pasture in a 5-gallon bucket. Then I'd run the sand through a strainer, sifting out the rocks. It was a decent bunker, with pretty white sand, but the cows took to lying in the bunker to beat the summer heat and I couldn't bring myself to chase them out.

In August, I withdrew another $1,000 to cover operating expenses and pay some bills. Then I took out another $2,000 to pay for the entry fee for the Senior PGA Tour qualifying. I had about

$5,800 left in the IRA and my intention was to make the money last at least through November 1995, giving me two shots at the Senior PGA Tour. Then I'd go look for a job—at a golf course or somewhere else. I figured having a track record as a professional golfer would look good to any prospective employer, inside the golf business or out.

Fortunately, I didn't have to make any more withdrawals from the IRA. In early October, I played in the Texoma Senior Open in Lawton, Oklahoma, a 36-hole event, and finished fifth. I shot 71-70/141, three-under, and saw that my game stacked up pretty well against the likes of Marty Fleckman, the former great touring pro from Texas, whom I figured to see again at Tour qualifying.

MY PAYDAY FOR THIRD-PLACE WAS $700—PUSHING MY CAREER EARNINGS AS A PRO TO NEARLY $1,000.

Before the tournament began, I flew up for a practice round with my friend Phil Lumsden, a really good amateur player who would be my partner at the Dallas Reunion Pro-Am in June. We went in Phil's little Cessna and it was my first time ever in a small private plane. I handled things all right, although Phil likes to joke that it took three days for the imprints of my fingers to pop out of the plane's dashboard. Okay, so I was holding on tight.

Lawton was a wide open golf course that was really easy from the tee. The greens were bentgrass and somewhat speedy. I played steady golf, but found myself to be a little more nervous and emotional than usual. Still, I kept my mistakes to to a minimum, and although I made only a few birdies in 54 holes, I hammered away with par after par. It wasn't spectacular golf, but it was solid. By the way, I talked Phil into driving up to Lawton for the tournament.

My payday for third-place was $700—pushing my career earnings as a pro golfer to nearly $1,000. I was so keyed up after that I could hardly sleep for the next week.

Meanwhile, Freddie was making career plans of her own. She said she was going to take her GED equivalency, so she could put that on an application when she went to look for a job, which she was planning to do, at Wal-Mart or somewhere like that.

Freddie had never finished high school, having been married at 15 and starting her family right after that. She went over to Weatherford Junior College and spent the whole day taking the test. She said everyone else in the room finished by noon, but she struggled right up to the final bell at 4 o'clock. She came home late that afternoon with a terrific headache and announced she was going straight to bed.

"Honey, how did you do on your test?" I wondered.

"Awful, Robert, just plain awful," she said. "I don't want to talk about it."

We didn't say another word about it, but Freddie was wrong about her performance. When we got the GED test results back a week or so later, she had passed with flying colors. Now she was feeling better about herself and suddenly had more confidence about re-entering the work force, which, because of my subsequent good fortune, she hasn't had to do.

When October rolled around, it was time for me to take my shot at big-time professional golf. I had the choice of four sites for Senior PGA Tour regional qualifying—Las Vegas, San Antonio and two places in Florida. I chose San Antonio, mainly because it was the closest to home. I drove down there and checked into a Motel 6 on the north side of town, not far from Woodlake Country Club. While I stayed at the course and practiced until dark each day, Tom Bodett left the light on for me.

The beauty of the San Antonio tournament, I discovered, was that we had 67 players in the field and a 60-man cut. That meant only seven players were going home after the first two rounds. I liked those odds. The other thing I liked was that the low 14 from the Texas qualifier had a history of faring pretty well at the national finals. If you had enough game to survive the regional qualifier in Texas, your chances of making it at national were at least decent and perhaps even pretty good.

The regional qualifier in San Antonio is like a fog bank in my memory. I see figures and shapes, but not many faces. I have very few specific memories, other than meeting a guy from South Bend,

Indiana named Jim Draskovitz. He's a nervous and energetic guy who really gets keyed up to play golf. If you had to plug me and most people in to recharge us at night, we would take 110 current; Jim, on the other hand, would need 220. He's not a long hitter, but he more than makes up for that with a great, short game.

I shot scores of 75-74-73-72, and that was good enough for ninth place in the field. I do remember that it helped me a great deal that my old friend, Rudy Belmares, who's the head pro at Mission Del Lago in San Antonio, let me come over to his course in the evening to practice putting. The practice green at Woodlake was so small and so crowded that I couldn't get in any quality work. You need a large practice green with plenty of slope, like the one at Mission Del Lago, to get anything accomplished. I owe Rudy a big debt of gratitude for that.

Anyway, we had only a week between the regional qualifier in San Antonio and the national qualifying tournament in Tampa. I needed to practice my golf, but I also had to keep up with firewood obligations. Like I said earlier, I was duty-bound to get wood to my customers.

I was cutting firewood that Sunday afternoon in a pretty dense grove of trees on my dad's 30 acres near Poolville. I was cutting on a dead tree, which had been struck by lightning, when I heard a loud "Moo." I didn't see anything, so I went to check the gate at the corner of the property, because the cows had knocked it down one time before.

I got in my pickup and drove to the back side of the farm, where suddenly I saw an old, familiar face. She came running up to me like a long-lost friend. I got out of the cab and gave her a big ol' squeeze.

I sped back home to tell Freddie the good news. "You'll never guess what just happened," I shouted, as I barged through the door. "I found Winnie!"

"What do mean you found Winnie?" cried Freddie. "Do you mean you found her bones?"

"No, I mean I found her," I explained. "She's big and fat and she's going to have a calf."

Freddie said, "Oh, Robert, are you sure it's Winnie?"

"Of course, I'm sure," I said. "She still has the nubby looking little horn," referring to the partial regrowth which had occured after she had been dehorned. There was no mistaking Winnie. We got a trailer and brought her home the next day.

Freddie and I were both tickled to death. Being reunited with Winnie was a miracle, because she'd been gone for six months. When one of your cattle has been missing for that length of time, generally that means it's gone for good.

Winnie wasn't the only cow that made a big impression on us the week before we went to Tampa. So did a little 500-pound calf named Sundance, who we were trying to wean from his mother, Casey. Casey is a high-spirited, though gentle, cow who is the leader of our herd. She's tan with a white face and 12 inch horns.

A few weeks earlier, before I went to San Antonio, it had come time to wean Sundance, so we herded him and three other calves into a small, reinforced pen with a 4 foot fence. If you don't have a pen like that, the calves will want their mothers and the mothers will want their calves. They'll do anything they can to get back together.

Just as we got the four calves in the weaning pen and shut the gate, we turned around to see Sundance clearing the fence, like a flat-footed high jumper. Fortunately, the weaning pen is inside a larger pen with an electric fence, which should have discouraged Sundance from making his escape. Unfortunately, Sundance hopped right over the electric fence as well, and kept right on going, rejoining the herd.

We kept the other three calves in the pen and sold them a few days later. Then Freddie and I figured out how to deal with Sundance, hatching a plan to close him up in our small, red barn, where there was no way out. Our plan was going smoothly. I was leading him in, and Freddie was to close the barn gate.

She was doing just that, slowly and carefully, when all of a sudden Sundance kicked out with his both back feet, like a mule, and hit the gate. The gate, in turn, hit Freddie flush in the face. The gate was made with 5/8 inch rods, and one of the rods caught Freddie square on the bridge of the nose.

Freddie knew at once her nose was broken. She was bleeding something awful. We got her cleaned up and bandaged, not able to afford a trip to the doctor just then, and we secured Sundance in the barn. The next day, my friend Lonnie Corley helped me haul Sundance over to the cattle sale in Weatherford. So long, Sundance.

I was afraid that the calf's temper tantrum had spelled an end to Freddie's plans to go with me to qualify in Tampa. Even though her face looked a mess, with black eyes and deep bruises, she wasn't about to miss out on the action. She put on some pancake make-up and wore dark sunglasses, and the farmers from Texas—Mister and Mrs.—drove down to Florida and had their day in the sun.

Freddie and I used to say that we were fairly unlucky people, but suddenly we didn't feel so unlucky any more. We realize now that we're two of the luckiest people in the world. Our prayers have been answered. The good Lord has been looking after us.

That's the message we want to share with people everywhere as we go on the Senior PGA Tour. Work hard, have patience, never stop believing in your dream—or yourself—and good things can happen to you, too. We're living proof of that.

Chapter Four

GROWING UP
COUNTRY

Let's go back to the beginning. Growing up as I did taught me that hard work, patience and believing in my dreams would pay off one day. I had no idea, however, the payoff would come in golf.

I was born in Fort Worth and raised in Tarrant County, near the town of Azle, which, according to the 1990 census, had a population of nearly 9,000. I've spent practically my whole life within a 25-mile radius of Fort Worth.

I was born January 6, 1944, in Harris Hospital in Fort Worth. I am a junior, named after my father, Robert Wayne Landers, Sr., who goes by Wayne. My mother was Ceila Lillie McDaniel. Our family, which included my sister, Lynna Kathleen, or Kathy, who was born in September 1946, lived on the Nine Mile Bridge Road, about a half mile off the Jacksboro Highway. Our house sat on one acre of land, five miles south of Azle.

My childhood memories are happy ones. I remember getting an electric train for Christmas when I was three or four, and a bicycle when I was six. My favorite activities were hunting and fishing. I got a BB gun when I was nine, and I had a hunting dog named Midget, who was part cocker spaniel. We were nearly inseparable, roaming around the countryside, flushing out birds.

When I started school, an old, rock building which housed all twelve grades, in Azle in 1950, I walked half a mile down to State Highway 199 to catch the bus. Though I walked by myself, when I got to the bus stop, there would be 10 to 15 kids there.

My first, close friend and classmate was Lonnie Roy Corley. We stayed friends throughout twelve grades of school, but lost track of each other after we graduated in 1962. Then in 1988, I discovered that Lonnie was renting a house across the creek from our farm, and we resumed our friendship.

At an early age, I developed a fascination with baseball. My father and I used to listen on the radio to the games of the Fort Worth Cats, the Texas League baseball club affiliated with the Brooklyn Dodgers. Every now and then, my dad would take the family to a Cats game at LaGrave Field on the north side of Fort Worth. My favorite player was Bobby Bragan, the Cats' manager and part-time catcher, who had been a major leaguer.

I had always wanted to catch a foul ball, or a home run, as a souvenir, but I never did. Sometimes in my dreams I wind up outside the outfield fence at some ballpark, where I find a bunch of baseballs or, for some reason, golf balls. The other kinds of dreams I have are about catching big catfish or playing impossible golf shots. I don't know what Dr. Sigmund Freud might interpret from those dreams.

Besides baseball, my other fascination was with nature. I have always loved to learn about birds and animals, and especially enjoy looking at pretty photographs of nature's creatures. I don't read much of anything at all, but I do enjoy looking at *Texas Parks and Wildlife* magazine. It's always been a favorite of mine.

This fascination with nature probably explains why I like to live in the woods and work in the dirt. My love for the outdoors may be one reason I find golf so appealing. Whatever the case, I find pleasure in cutting brush, trimming trees, chopping firewood and shoveling gravel from creek beds. I don't cut big, pretty trees when I cut firewood, I trim and cut damaged trees. I don't cut hollow trees or stumps, because they are someone's home.

My father was away serving in the U.S. Navy, during World War II, when I was born. He never talked much about combat, but he told me once about being part of the Normandy invasion on D-Day, June 6, 1944, five months to the day after I was born.

He said he saw hundreds of men being killed as the Allies assaulted the beaches. It was a terrible experience, and he swore right then and there that if he ever got back home alive, he would dedicate his life to the Lord and be the best person he possibly could be. He kept his word, too.

This is one reason that my recollection of my early years is having grown up in a tranquil, Ozzie and Harriet-type home. We always had whatever we needed, but never any more. Our home life was simple and quiet.

My parents were very thrifty people who believed in saving. Their needs and tastes were simple. My dad was a government meat inspector with the United States Department of Agriculture. His job was to inspect the cattle, goats, sheep and hogs before they were slaughtered. Later, he moved up to inspect the steaks and other meat products. I remember him working at the Swift and Armour packing plants in Fort Worth and having to get up at 4:30 A.M. to work the second or third shift. My mother drove him to work on the days she needed the family car. I remember we had an old Kaiser. Later, we got a 1951 Studebaker.

MY PARENTS WERE VERY THRIFTY PEOPLE WHO BELIEVED IN SAVING. THEIR NEEDS AND TASTES WERE SIMPLE.

My parents were also devout Christians, members of the Church of Christ. They believed in walking the straight and narrow, and their everyday lives reflected those beliefs. They raised me and my sister the same way.

Our family life revolved around going to church. We never missed going even once that I can remember, attending Sunday morning, school and service, Sunday evening and Wednesday night. The first church I can remember was the Old Bluff Springs schoolhouse. Later, we changed to the New Bluff Springs Church of Christ, which my dad and his brothers built on an acre of land donated by my grandmother Edna, Granny Landers.

We attended these tiny country churches that had maybe 20 or 30 members. Half or more of the people in the congregation were my kinfolks, one way or the other. My mother used to say that she wished we could go to a larger church, so Kathy and I could be around more young people and have more activities.

My mother was a gifted person. She was an artist with both music and paint. She played the piano, and for all the years I can remember, she gave lessons to kids in the Azle area. That was her way of contributing to the family income. Again, my parents made sure that Kathy and I had whatever we needed growing up, but we didn't have any luxuries, like money for taking trips or acquiring many worldly things.

My parents both came from large families and both sets of my grandparents were poor working people who never had a debt they didn't pay. My mother was the oldest of six McDaniel children. My father was the next-to-youngest of nine Landers children. They knew what it was like to grow up in the Depression as part of large working families on the farm. They were honest, religious, devout Christians, who lived ordinary lives.

As you might suppose, growing up in this environment, I had an extremely sheltered childhood. I received only the information necessary to get by on a day-to-day basis. Therefore, if I didn't learn things at school—and I was no great shakes as a student—I didn't learn them at all.

I also spent a lot of time alone, or with Midget, which probably accounts for why, years later, I would enjoy the solitude of hitting golf balls. When you think about it, golf is a pretty lonely sport. To improve your game, you must invest a lot of time working by yourself.

I had some, good friends growing up—just not many of them. Lonnie Corley lived with his grandparents three-quarters of a mile from me, and I went to his house to play a few times. He came to my house probably four times as often. Another friend was Paul James Farley, or Jimmy, who moved into Uncle Tommy McDaniel's house next door when I was in the third grade.

Jimmy Farley was a well-mannered, well-raised boy. His dad was a dedicated family man, who worked at Convair and later at the post office in Fort Worth. His mom was a housewife, who raised Jimmy and three other kids.

Jimmy had polio as a young boy and, because of his illness, I could outrun, outkick and outthrow him, and though he was a year older, I was also a better shot. I figured out, years later, that Jimmy had a dominant left eye and should have been shooting BB guns lefthanded, not righthanded. Anyway, Jimmy was a real competitor, who played hard, whether he won or lost. We played a lot together, and he was a good friend.

My only other friend, who lived nearby, about three-quarters of a mile away through the woods on the next road was Mike Vaughan. He moved to the area when we were in the fourth grade. Mike was the next-to-youngest of five Vaughan kids, and he liked to hang around close to home. Though we were good friends from the beginning, we became very close in later years.

Being a country kid, I took an immediate interest in guns. When I was really little, I asked my mom how to spell "BB", so I could ask Santa Claus for a BB gun for Christmas. I didn't get one, however, until I was nine. My dad didn't own a gun of any kind, so naturally he was in no hurry to get me one.

I carried that BB gun around for nearly six years, shooting at anything that moved. Once I got into a pitched BB gun battle with Jimmy Farley's cousins, Wayne and Ronnie Norris. Jimmy ran home and told my mother what was happening before we could do any serious damage, like put out an eye.

My next step up in arms came at age 15, when I got a Mossberg Model 183, a 410 Bolt Action, Single Shot Shotgun. I knew I had arrived as an outdoorsman. Over the years, I have collected anything that had to do with guns—empty shot shell cases, brass cases, lead and so on. I started loading ammo at 15, after finding out quickly that I couldn't feed my Mossberg without reloading.

As the years have gone by, my interest has settled on high velocity small caliber rifles—.220 Swift is my current favorite. It's funny, I suppose, that I have never collected golf clubs or golf stuff, but I can't part with any gun. I've been a member of the National Rifle Association (NRA) since I was 16 years old, and have always enjoyed flipping through *American Riflemen*.

People who ask me what I'm going to do with the money I make on the Senior PGA Tour probably expect to hear that I want a new Mercedes or a big, fancy house, something like that. Actually, about the only things I'd be interested in acquiring would be more guns or a flugelhorn.

A flugelhorn might strike some people as a strange thing to wish for, but before I became a golfer, I was a musician. I must have inherited a gene for music from my mother, who started me playing the piano at an early age. My sister and I even played piano duets at recitals.

When I was in the sixth grade, my parents bought me an Olds Ambassador trumpet. Through junior high and high school, the trumpet became the tool with which I was going to make my mark. I easily excelled in music at school, mainly because I had the advantage of getting private lessons on a weekly basis for the next few years. One of my parents would drive me over to the River Oaks section of Fort Worth for lessons with Mr. Ken Foler, a very well-rounded musician and teacher.

I learned later on that I had a pretty good ear (though shooting guns so much had diminished that ability somewhat), but I was a poor sight reader. That alone kept me from being anything special beyond high school, where I could always memorize my part.

One of the things I liked about living in the country was that I had the freedom to play my trumpet whenever the mood hit. I'd often sit outside, or wander around under a starry Texas sky, playing some of my favorite songs like "Blue Moon," "Stardust," "Somewhere Over the Rainbow" and "Cherry Pink (And Apple Blossom White)." Another one of my favorites was Doris Day's hit, "Secret Love." I'd also practice John Philip Sousa marches and other songs we played in the Azle High School marching band.

I turned a deaf ear on the rock-and-roll craze that was sweeping the nation back in the late 1950s and early 1960s. Guys like Elvis Presley, Ricky Nelson, Pat Boone, Buddy Holly, Roy Orbison—all that stuff meant nothing to me. I didn't take much interest in automobiles, like a lot of guys did, either. I guess I was too accustomed to going places on foot. I'd rather spend an afternoon roaming the country with my gun than working under the hood of a '57 Chevy.

I was in no big hurry to get a driver's license either. Most Texas teenagers, in those days, were lined up at the Texas Highway Patrol Office on the morning they turned 16. Many of them had been driving illegally for a couple years. I didn't even bother applying for my license until six months after my 16th birthday. Cars didn't have much of a place in my narrow world.

Besides the marching band, I also played in Azle High's stage-band, which was directed by Greg Berry. He came into Azle my last year in high school and really made a difference in the community over the next few years, getting kids entered in regional and state band competitions. Our stage band made appearances on holidays and at special, school assemblies. Not long ago, I heard from the daughter of Jimmy Hagler, our drummer, who's now living in California. He'd heard about me qualifying for the Senior PGA Tour and, for good luck, he made me a horseshoe putter. It's the darnedest thing to see, with a horseshoe where the head of the club should be. I need to thank him for that.

After finishing high school in Azle in May 1962, I enrolled five days later at Texas Christian University in Fort Worth as a music education major. I chose TCU for no particular reason, other than my first-cousin, Janice Newsom, who was then attending Texas Tech in Lubbock, probably said something like "Oh, Robert, you ought to go TCU."

Like I've been trying to say, I was pretty naive and impressionable. I had no driving ambition in life, but I figured I could play, or learn to play, the trumpet well enough to become a professional musician. After three years, however, I realized I would never be a really good trumpet player. One thing that brought me to this realization was hearing a fellow TCU student named Ronnie Puckett play. He was a world beater, and, to this day, the best trumpet player I have ever heard.

As I mentioned earlier, besides guns and trumpets, my other great passion was baseball. When I reached junior high, I wanted to play on the baseball team, but I soon found out Azle didn't have one. The high school coach wanted athletics focused on two things—football and track. Basketball served primarily to keep kids in shape for track, and track served mainly to get kids' legs in shape for football. That's how high school sports are in many small Texas towns like Azle: Everything revolves around football.

In the seventh grade, I skipped football and played my trumpet in the band. In the eighth grade, I tried out for the football team. After two days of practice, the coach posted a list of names on a door and announced, "If your name is on the list, you can play on the team."

I checked the list of names and didn't see mine. I didn't ask the coach why I'd been cut. I thought to myself, "Oh, well, if you can't play this year, you can try again next year." I went back to the band and played trumpet.

When ninth grade came around, I tried out for football again. This time, I made the team. The coach said, "Robert, why didn't you try out last year?" I said, "I did, but my name wasn't on the list, so I figured I wasn't good enough to play."

The coach said, "Son, you should have asked about it."

I just couldn't bring myself to ask such things. I don't know why, but, to this day, I have difficulty asking questions, speaking to people or even doing something as simple as making a telephone call. I'm getting better at it, with all the interviews and appearances

I DON'T THINK I WAS THE BEST PUNTER WE HAD, BUT ALL I CAN FIGURE IS THAT BECAUSE I PRACTICED SO MUCH, THE COACH THOUGHT I'D BE MORE CONSISTENT THAN THE OTHER GUYS.

necessary in my new career as a professional golfer, but it's never been easy for me to do.

I didn't ever get into a football game in the ninth grade, maybe because I only weighed about 95 pounds and the coach probably figured I'd get squashed. In the tenth grade, I made the Azle High "B" team and played about one-quarter of the time. I was always very timid, though, afraid of getting hurt. My mom was also afraid. I guess that was the reason I was so tentative about contact.

In my junior year of high school, I was designated as the team's punter. I believe the reason was because the coach had asked the players to train during the summer, and I had gone up to the school on a weekly basis and lifted weights and run the stadium and bleachers.

Because I was by myself a good bit, either at home or up at the school, I kicked a lot of footballs. I don't think I was the best punter we had, but all I can figure is that because I practiced so much, the coach thought I'd be more consistent than the other guys. He gave me the job.

It was a short season, however. After the fourth game, while playing football at home with Jimmy Farley and his brother, Mike, I cut my knee open pretty badly on a piece of glass. The injury caused me to see limited action the rest of the year, and I didn't earn a varsity letter. It was very close, but I didn't quite qualify.

During my senior year in high school, I had filled out to a strapping 140 pounds, and I started on defense and played occasionally on offense as a receiver. My most embarrassing moment came when I was wide open in the secondary. Someone had busted an assignment and there was no defender within ten yards—and I dropped an easy pass. The coach immediately sent in a replacement, and I trotted back over to the sideline.

The coach waved me over to him and got in my face. "Son," he said, "Didn't you want to catch that pass?"

What could I say? "I wanted to, coach," I told him. "But I just didn't do it."

My one moment of glory in high school football came in the game against Brewer High. I caught two touchdown passes from Mark Myers, the only times I ever found the end zone. I don't remember any of the Azle cheerleaders coming up to hug me after the game, or anything special like that.

But then I never had much to do with girls when I was growing up. I went through my high school years without even having a single date. When I was 14, I developed my first crush. Her name was Barbara Simpson and she was 10 years old. She and her brothers, Richard and Joe, and her cousins, Pat and Judy Mason, came to our house twice a week for piano lessons.

I was attracted to Barbara immediately, but for years after, I was too insecure to muster the courage to tell her that I liked her, or, when we got older, to ask her for a date. Our mothers did arrange for Barbara to accompany me to a banquet during my senior year in high school, probably so I wouldn't have to go alone. One other time, Barbara went with me on a band trip to Forest Park in Fort Worth, but I wouldn't call those real dates.

The Azle Hornets had a strong football program under head football coach, Don Hood. In the late 1950s and early 1960s, we won the district championship several times in a row. It wasn't that we were better athletes than our opponents. It was that we were better conditioned and better motivated by Coach Hood and his staff.

I can honestly say that Coach Don Hood is the one person who had the most influence on the rest of my life. The things Coach Hood taught his football players about how they should live their lives have stuck with me all these years. His philosophy matched the way I was raised by my parents and squared with my home life.

Coach Hood insisted that anyone who played on any of his teams had to walk a straight line. There was no smoking, drinking, cussing, or staying out late at night. He also taught us that if you worked hard enough at anything you do, you could be as good as anybody. Coach Hood's message became the key to my later success in golf: I had put in years of hard work, and had reaped the benefits.

Others who shaped my development in sports were Allen Merrett, one of Coach Hood's assistant football coaches, and two Azle residents, Billy Bob Irby, a bricklayer, and Burn C. Moody, a postman, who coached my youth baseball teams. Again, the major disappointment of my teenage years was the lack of an organized baseball program in Azle.

My experiences with athletics in Azle would later have a big impact on my career in golf. Although my first love was baseball, growing up in the country made it difficult to find anyone around to play catch with or to pitch me batting practice. You need at least a dozen other kids around to have a decent game of baseball, but in golf all you need is a club and a ball. I suppose I probably put some of my love for hitting a baseball into hitting a golf ball.

Next to Coach Don Hood, Phil Henderson probably has had the most profound influence on my life. Phil, who is five years older than I am was another great friend from my childhood years. Sharing an interest in hunting, fishing and guns, he became sort of the big brother I never had. He was strong, smart, honest and loyal and his goodness, moral fiber and kindness toward me have always been beyond question.

I shared some great adventures with Phil. We'd go hunting, and even if he had only one bullet for his rifle, he'd let me take the shot. We hunted deer, doves, quail, squirrels, snakes, and bullfrogs.

When I dropped out of TCU, after my junior year—Ronnie Puckett and his trumpet having blown a hole in my plans to become a musician, in addition to my not being "modern" enough for modern jazz—Phil arranged for me to get a job at Jay Needham Refrigeration Manufacturing Company in Fort Worth.

At Needham, we built panels for walk-in coolers and freezers. No one in the shop could come close to keeping up with Phil, who is the hardest working guy I have ever met. With a hammer and nail, he is an absolute wizard. He could seat a 16 penny nail with two licks. What's more, he didn't miss.

One thing that Phil taught me—something his father had taught him—was that if you're hunting, you're hunting. If you're fishing, you're fishing. If you're building panels, you're building panels. You can only do one thing at a time, so be sure you do it right and with all your effort.

I put Phil Henderson's advice to use when I took up golf. My attitude became when you're playing golf, you're playing golf. You don't horse around, or goof off, or give it less than your all.

In addition to Phil's advice about doing everything with a single-minded purpose, the words of encouragement and inspiration that came from Coach Don Hood, all those years ago, still reverberate in my mind like a trumpet solo. Coach Hood told the Azle Hornets that we had a chance to become champions, which we did, but that, in order to do so, we had to work harder and smarter than the competition. I bought into his every word.

When I started playing golf in the mid-1960s, Coach Hood's message—work harder and smarter—became my personal creed. In making the effort to improve, I discovered something that is true in football, golf or any other endeavor you undertake in life: If you aren't willing to pay the price in preparation, you can't expect to see any achievement, or success.

Chapter Five

BITTEN BY THE
GOLF BUG

I remember the summer of 1965 as one of the happiest times of my life. By day, I was earning a steady paycheck at Needham Refrigeration, where I worked with my buddy Phil Henderson. By night, I was going out with my first love, Barbara Simpson. I had called her one day that spring, right before I left TCU, and found out that she was going through a divorce. I knew this was my one chance to have a relationship with the woman of my dreams, and I was doing my best to make the most of it.

Little did I know I was on the threshold of a fateful event that would change my life forever: I was about to be introduced to the game of golf.

To celebrate the end of summer, my relatives got together in Fort Worth at my Grandmother McDaniel's house for a big Labor Day reunion and cookout. Mamaw's house was full with aunts, uncles and cousins, some of whom I didn't know all that well. There was enough food—fried chicken, ham, turkey, mashed potatoes and yams, cole slaw, homemade ice cream—to feed an Army platoon.

Foster Stevens, who lived in Wichita Falls and who was married to my mother's sister, Ruby McDaniel, came up to me after everyone had finished eating lunch, and said "Robert, I'm going to teach you how to play golf."

"That sounds great, Uncle Foster," I said. "What do we do?"

At the time, I knew next to nothing about golf. For all I knew, Ben Hogan was the star of "Hogan's Heroes" on TV. And Juan Rodriguez was a waiter at Joe T. Garcia's, the famous Fort Worth Tex-Mex restaurant. I had heard of Arnold Palmer, like everybody else, but I'm not sure I had heard of Jack Nicklaus, even though by then he had already won The Masters and the U.S. Open, replacing Palmer as the best golfer in the world.

To be honest, I thought golf was a game only rich people played. And I'd never known any rich people, with the exception of Uncle Wilburn. Wilburn Newsom was married to my mother's sister, Lena, and was an executive with Mitchell's Department Stores.

Uncle Foster led me out into the front yard and showed me how to hold a golf club with an interlocking grip. It's the same grip I use today, nearly 30 years later. We chipped a few balls around the lawn, and the next thing I knew Uncle Foster decided we should drive over to Rockwood Park. There we hit a bucket of balls at the driving range and then, at Uncle Foster's urging and expense, we hacked around for 9 holes.

I don't remember what we shot that day, but I do remember having a great time. I really enjoyed the sunshine, fresh air and the sheer physical pleasure associated with smacking that little dimpled white ball. I also remember asking him, before he headed home to Wichita Falls, where he worked as a service manager for Burroughs, "Tell me, Uncle Foster, how do you swing the club hard and still manage to hit the ball?" I've forgotten his exact reply.

The golf bug had bitten me. Hard! I had no idea that I was about to devote the next 30 years of life to golf, but not long after that I scurried over to Montgomery Ward on 7th Street in Fort Worth and fished a Patty Berg model ladies' 8-iron out of a barrel of clubs. I paid $3 for it. I rounded up 13 old golf balls from somewhere and hit those balls until their covers practically came off.

The next club I acquired was a Billy Casper driver, which I purchased at Ward's for $10. Then I began spending time in the neighborhood park hitting the driver in one direction and hitting back with my 8-iron. Later, I added a Wilson R90 Sand Wedge, rounding out my three-club set. I began hitting balls in city parks or fields every chance I could. What was funny was that I never lost any golf balls. I just kept finding more, adding to my collection.

It may sound like I was a disadvantaged golfer, having only three clubs at my disposal. But, looking back, that might have been a blessing, because I'd didn't have to decide between 14 clubs in my bag, or try to give equal attention to all of them.

By hitting my driver so much, I became relatively comfortable with the most critical shot in golf, the one that sets up every par-4 or par-5 hole. And having only two irons to hit, I practiced how to hit different shots. I experimented with hooding the club on some shots, leaving it open and cutting the ball on others. I remember doing a lot of cutting in those early weeks and months, because like most beginners, I had problems with a big slice.

*

I BEGAN HITTING BALLS IN CITY PARKS OR FIELDS EVERY CHANCE I COULD. WHAT WAS FUNNY WAS THAT I NEVER LOST ANY GOLF BALLS.

It also probably helped in the long run that I hit so many balls with the sand wedge. That's the main scoring club in the bag, the one you use from 100 yards in. I think golfers should spend at least 50 percent of their practice time using just the sand wedge. Hitting shots from 50, 60 or 70 yards helps you develop feel and touch.

I wasn't content to stay a three-clubber for long, however. Late in 1965, I went to Leonard's Department Store and bought a half set (3/5/7/9 and putter) of Wilson irons. As I recall, they were Julius Boros models, but I can't remember how much they cost. Later I would add a McGregor 6-iron, a Wilson 4-iron and Northwestern 2-iron. I put together, to say the least, a mixed bag.

In addition to being a new golfer, I had become a married golfer. Barbara accepted my proposal, and we were married on

November 18, 1965 at the Bluff Springs Church of Christ in Azle. We couldn't afford a honeymoon, so we didn't take one.

Everything in my life seemed to be going along pretty well, until one day in early 1966, when I got a letter from the U.S. Government with my draft notice enclosed. I immediately decided to go down to the U.S. Air Force recruiting office in Fort Worth and enlist. The date was February 6, 1966. I went through six months of training at Lackland Air Force Base in San Antonio and Chanute Air Force Base in Champaign, Illinois.

At Chanute, I completed training to become a jet engine mechanic. When the school was finished, everyone waited to receive orders. Many expected to be one-way tickets to Vietnam. I had written "Texas" as the duty station on my "wish list," and was praying that I'd be assigned somewhere close to home.

I got even more than I had hoped for. When my orders arrived, one of my roommates, a guy from Oregon named Denova, called out: "Hey, Robert. Have you ever heard of an air base called Carswell?"

"Certainly, man," I shot back. "That's in Fort Worth. You know that's where I'm from."

"Well, guess what, pal," Denova said. "You're going home."

"That's not even funny," I told him. "That's a bad joke. You shouldn't tease a guy about something like that."

"No, man, I'm serious," he said. "Your orders are up and that's where you're going."

I said, "Since I've been here, nobody has ever been sent to Carswell. Not one person. Sorry, but I don't believe you."

So Denova showed me the orders and there it was, bigger than life: Airman Robert Landers, blah-blah-blah, report to Carswell AFB, Fort Worth, Texas.

By August 1966, I was back home in Tarrant County. I was a slick-sleeved airman, meaning I had no stripes, the lowest rank in the Air Force's pecking order. I repaired J-57 jet engines for B-52 bombers and KC 135 tankers. My pay was $300 a month.

I remember that not long after I got there, another slick sleeve showed up. The first sergeant, who was boss in the shop, looked over our new arrival and wasn't too impressed.

"Hey, are you a slick sleeve fresh out of basic training?" asked the first sergeant.

"Hell, no," came the reply. "I'm a slick sleeve fresh out of jail."

Everyone in the shop had a big laugh over that, especially the first sergeant. That was one of the best things the old sarge could have heard, because it meant he had a well-experienced hand. Sarge was tickled pink to have the guy, because the shop was always running behind schedule.

Anyway, the slick sleeve made sergeant right quick and later got promoted to crew chief. I worked for him for about a year or so and he taught me a lot about jet engines. I'm just sorry I can't remember his name. He was a good man.

When the Labor Day weekend came around in 1966, Uncle Foster drove down from Wichita Falls again for our annual family gathering, and we resumed our golf sessions. We went back to Rockwood Park and I got in my first regulation 18 holes of golf. I shot 96, which Uncle Foster said was pretty good for a first-timer. All I remember was hitting a lot of crooked shots.

About six weeks later, on October 22, 1966, Barbara gave birth to Robert Wayne Landers III. Nearly two years later, on August 11, 1968, Barbee Landers joined our family. By then, we were living in River Oaks near the base, in a house we purchased in 1967.

I was stationed at Carswell AFB from August 1966 to August 1969, and during this period I learned how to play golf. My first year at Carswell I didn't play the base course very much. It was too tough. Instead, I practiced in the city parks, played the Rockwood par-3 course at night and played at Rockwood Park municipal golf course every now and then.

I kept to myself mostly, partly because of insecurity and partly because I didn't know anyone else who played golf. But then in 1967, my dad began playing golf, and at least I had a regular playing partner.

The golf course at Rockwood Park is pretty easy, a good place for beginners to get started in golf. It's fairly flat and wide open and there's not too much water, sand or other kinds of trouble to negotiate.

The golf course at Carswell, on the other hand, is difficult, with plenty of trees and water and some tight driving holes. The course teaches you to avoid all the trouble—or pay a stiff price. It forces you to learn to manage your game. Course management later would become one of the strengths of my game, and I owe a lot of that to learning on a tough layout like Carswell.

I spent the last six months of my Air Force duty overseas (Barbara and the kids stayed in Fort Worth), after the 7th Bomb Wing was sent TDY (temporary duty) to U Taphao, a base on the Gulf of Thailand, about 100 miles south of Bangkok. They were fly-ing about 60 bombing missions a day, and 90 refueling missions, with the KC-135s.

It was a busy outfit. Guys would work a rotation of five days on and one day off, then seven days on and one day off. I remem-ber one guy in the wing named Lamb, who was always organizing trips down to the NCO club. He'd get a bunch of guys from the bar-racks to go with him and they'd whoop it up pretty good. The next morning, they'd come trooping into work with nasty hangovers. Then somebody would ask "Where's Lamb?" and everyone sudden-ly realized it was his day off. Lamb pulled that one off several times.

On my days off, I would hit golf balls at the base driving range. Once or twice, I went out and played a new golf course in the area that had been roughly hewn out of the forest. But it was a cab ride away and, besides, any time you left the base, you might be asking for trouble.

By the time I mustered out of the Air Force in early 1970, my golf handicap was down to around 5. I still wasn't a real solid ball-striker, like a lot of 5-handicap golfers are, but I knew how to avoid trouble and manage myself around a golf course. That is something a lot of 10-15 handicaps should attempt to do to improve: concen-trate on making smart, safe plays rather than going for great shots.

Anyway, I went to work for American National Insurance Co. in Fort Worth, doing something I was neither prepared for, nor well-equipped, to handle. I was a debit agent, meaning I had my own route and went door to door collecting on insurance policies and trying to sell new ones. Needless to say, I didn't have the outgoing personality or the self-confidence you need to succeed in selling insurance.

I worked at American National for a guy named Bob Lee, who played golf with me and my dad, and another guy named E.O. Meyer, every Saturday at the old Singin' Hills golf course on the western outskirts of Fort Worth. Bob Lee once told me that if I put the effort into selling insurance that I put into golf, I could become a pretty good insurance agent. What's more, Lee told me that I would never be a good golfer. Hearing his remark really stung me, and gave me added determination to be a successful amateur player. I was determined to prove him wrong.

With all the practice time I was putting in, during lunch and after work, I was making steady progress with my game. The first really good round I ever had (also the first time I broke par) came on the front nine at Rockwood Park late in 1970. I remember being two-under through eight holes and facing a chip on number nine from the front of the green. I hit to three feet and realized that even if I two-putted, I would break par for the first time in my life. A sense of great joy swept over me. I made the putt and shot 33.

Then one day in 1971, Uncle Wilburn Newsom invited me to play with him at the Ridglea Country Club championship course. It's a tough layout, which requires plenty of length from the tee, and I guess I was inspired by being on such a good course. I had my best round ever, a two-under par 70. After the round, either as a reward for my good play or an incentive for me to keep improving, Uncle Wilburn loaned me his McGregor irons. They became my first matched set, replacing the Wilsons I'd bought at Leonard's back in 1965. Not long after, Uncle Wilburn bought a new set of clubs and this time he loaned me his Haig Ultras. With my new equipment, I thought I was in tall cotton.

After two years of struggling in the insurance business, I finally decided to go into another line of work. Not being able to go out and look for employment with any degree of confidence, I went to see Uncle Wilburn and asked for a job. By then he was the president and part-owner of Mitchell Department Stores, which, in 1972, had something like 72 stores across Texas. I guess it wasn't too hard for him to find a place to put me.

The first year I spent in a manager trainee program and things went well, although I didn't have much time for golf. Which may have been a blessing, because I probably needed a little rest to recharge my battery.

WHEN WE ADDED UP THE SCORES, I HAD SHOT A 66. MY MITCHELL'S COLLEAGUES COULDN'T BELIEVE IT. NEITHER COULD I.

What I remember most about 1972, though, was that my mother passed away that year from stomach cancer. In the fall of 1971, she had developed, out of the blue, a problem with her digestion. Every time she tried to eat, she had trouble keeping down her food. Her doctor, Dr. Leroy Bursey, went in to perform exploratory surgery and no more than 30 minutes later he came out to the waiting room and told my dad and me that my mother had stomach cancer and it was far beyond any possible treatment, period. Dr. Bursey told us she had maybe six weeks to live.

We were devastated, of course. None of us had a hint of how serious things were. We got to visit her later that day, and one of the first things she told us was that she knew the doctor hadn't done much, because she felt too good when she woke up.

My mother lived for another six months, staying at home where my dad could look after her. She never went back to the hospital again. One of her dying requests was that my father get remarried (which he did, to Evelyn Main, about seven months later). She also said her deepest regret in life would be not getting to see her grandchildren (my kids, Robert III and Barbee, and Kathy's son, Richard Scott Moreland) grow up. Mom died at home on February 8, 1972 at the age of 55. She was buried in the Greenwood Cemetery in Fort Worth.

In January 1973, I got my first store manager's job in the White Settlement area of Fort Worth, at the Cherry Lane store. That was also the first year that I started getting into a specific practice routine. I couldn't afford greens fees, but I went to a little park on the outskirts of Benbrook, where Barbara and I had bought a home, and hit balls every day. I could see continued improvement in my ball striking. As I made better contact with the ball, my distances with each club improved, and so did my confidence.

One day in the spring of 1973, I met some of the other Mitchell's people at the municipal course over in Grand Prairie. For some strange reason, I could do nothing wrong. Typical of my shots that day was a 9-iron to the par-3 on the 17th hole, which covered the flag the whole way and looked like it might go in. The ball stopped five feet short and I sank the birdie putt. When we added up the scores, I had shot a 66. My Mitchell's colleagues couldn't believe it. Neither could I.

Driving home to Fort Worth, I contemplated my good fortune and decided that that one 18-hole round had demonstrated how rewards are passed out in golf. I realized that if you stick with something long enough, that if you practice daily and control yourself, that someday something good will happen to you.

You won't know when or where, because that is definitely out of your control. And it doesn't matter how hard you try or how bad you want something, there is no guarantee anywhere for anything. But somewhere, some day, something good will happen. All it takes is patience.

Something else that I started doing from that day on was keeping a log. Every time I went out to play, I wrote down the results of the round. I kept statistics on fairways hit, length of putts made, successful up-and-downs, and so on. Each month I would average out the statistics to see where I was the most deficient and what areas of my game needed the most work. I also tried to identify, and eliminate, my most costly mistakes.

By early 1973, I had started playing the ball down exclusively, meaning I didn't roll it over to improve the lie. I adopted the attitude that it was okay to sacrifice, if you had to, for a bad or poor lie. One of the rules I learned to play by is "The lie of the ball tells you what you can and can't do with the shot." In other words, a golfer must learn to recognize how the ball lies, so you can make the best decision to give yourself the best chance to hit a successful shot. You have to make the percentages work in your favor.

I believe strongly that this is something golfers must learn to do, but it seems almost against human nature to use good judgment. Golfers always want to hit spectacular shots, every time. Most of the time, on the municipal courses I play, you can't have that attitude and be a good player.

That brings to mind a direction golf has gone that I believe hurts the individual player—scrambles. Nowadays, almost all tournaments have a scramble format, where all the players in a group hit the same shot and then you pick the best one. This format makes poor players out of average players, and average players out of good players.

Scrambles are great for players who don't hit the ball well and need to lean on another (better) player. But once someone can break 80, he needs to work on playing the ball down (which he never does), on managing the course (which he never does) and on hitting good, safe shots (which he never does).

Scrambles encourage players to hit the ball harder than they really can, and to hit one unsuccessful shot after another, while trying to hit that one great shot. When I hit a spectacular shot, it is usually an accident, because I am probably trying to put the ball in one area, rather than at the pin. While playing scrambles, the golfer is just trying to do the impossible.

The one good thing about scrambles, though, is that they have introduced countless more players to the game of golf. So scrambles aren't all bad. Just mostly!

Anyway, 1973 would prove to be the year that validated all my efforts to improve. I practiced all summer, pointing toward the Fort Worth City Championship at Pecan Valley, scheduled for Labor Day weekend. The tournament dates coincided with the eighth anniversary of when my introduction to golf by Uncle Foster.

The city championship that year taught me that if a person is patient, he can attain his just rewards, especially if your expectations aren't too high.

The first round at Pecan Valley I shot 71, which tied my best score ever on that golf course. The second round I shot 72, which put me in the final group for the last day. I played with John Granger and Russell Noblett, who were just at the end of their college careers, and Phil Lumsden.

The final day I shot 69, breaking 70 at Pecan Valley for the first time, and finished in third place behind Granger and Noblett. That one taste of success whet my appetite for competitive golf. I promised myself to practice harder than ever, and set the goal of returning the next Labor Day and winning the tournament.

Setting goals is another key part in successful golf. Too many golfers play the game too casually, without setting specific performance targets for themselves. The only way to improve in golf is to set realistic goals, and then see if you can attain them. The goal of winning the Fort Worth City Championship, which seemed realistic after my success in 1973, fueled my desire to improve.

Chapter Six

GETTIN IN A GROOVE

In January 1974, I was named manager of the Mitchell's store in Azle. I had not visited my hometown very often since leaving for TCU in the fall of 1962, but I soon discovered that things hadn't changed all that much. Azle was still mostly a bedroom community for people who worked in Fort Worth, and I still knew many of the residents and merchants. Everybody in town made me feel right at home. Barbara and I kept our home in Benbrook, and I made the 46-mile round trip drive to Azle every Monday through Saturday.

There were still no golf courses, or driving ranges, in Azle. It became my custom to hit golf balls during my lunch hour. Folks must have thought it pretty strange to see the new manager of Mitchell's standing out in a city park, or in an empty field, near where the Azle library now stands, hitting balls and tramping through the grass to collect them all.

I was doing all that practicing with the single goal of winning the Fort Worth City Tournament in September. I bought my first full set of golf clubs that year—Wilson 1200s, woods and irons, with stiff shafts. I paid $400 for those clubs, and played with them for the next five years. Then I gave them to my son.

Shortly after I returned to Azle, a guy named B.J. Clark, who owned Clark's Guns and Ammo, asked me to join the Sertoma Club. I had heard of this organization a few years earlier, because the downtown Fort Worth Sertoma Club sponsors an annual golf tournament.

At B.J.'s invitation, or maybe I should say his insistence, I went to a meeting of the Azle Sertoma Club and agreed, reluctantly, to join. As I've mentioned, I was not especially comfortable around strangers and have had a problem with being in new places and trying to function with other people.

I soon learned, however, everyone in Sertoma accepted me and that I could participate without being self-conscious. Pretty soon, I started volunteering for projects and committees. This greatly helped me function with other people in an open and positive manner. I even served two terms as president of Sertoma in the late 1970s.

I felt like a new man. For the first time in my life, I could get up in front of a crowd and speak. I was able to greet strangers and sell myself to them. I didn't feel the self-conscious embarrassment, the insecurity and lack of confidence, that I had always felt before in such circumstances. Through Sertoma, I had found an inner strength previously lacking in my life.

Our goal in the Sertoma Club, which was founded in Kansas City in 1912 and which has chapters all over the country, is to help people who need help. Our specialty is working with people who have speech and hearing problems. We have participated in many other programs and projects through the years and have helped many Azle citizens. I'm proud to have Sertoma's emblem on my golf bag, and I hope to spread the word about Sertoma everywhere I go on the Senior PGA Tour in 1995.

Besides Sertoma, I also became involved with the Azle Golf Association, a group of guys interested in golf who tried to play one tournament a month. I was the tournament coordinator for awhile, meaning my job was to call one of the local courses around Azle or Fort Worth on Monday morning and get tee times for the following weekend, and then let all the members know what had been set up.

My problem was getting off work to play. Most of the time, I tried to schedule tee times on Sunday, to make sure I could participate, but a lot of the members preferred playing on Saturday, when I had to work at Mitchell's, so I probably only played about half the time.

Through the Azle Golf Association, I met one of my best friends in golf, Keith Flatt. He's the son of Helen Vaughan, the older sister of my childhood friend, Mike Vaughan. The first time I played golf with Keith was at Lake Country Golf Club, on Eagle Mountain Lake, in an Azle Golf Association event.

On that particular day, the weather was cold and the wind was blowing and our scores were nothing special. But Keith and I formed an immediate friendship. I remember he wasn't a long hitter, which he later became, but he hit the ball straight down the middle.

> *
>
> **OUR GOAL IN**
>
> **THE SERTOMA**
>
> **CLUB IS TO**
>
> **HELP PEOPLE**
>
> **WHO NEED HELP.**

A year or so later, Keith caddied for me in the U.S. Open Qualifying at Ridglea Country Club in Fort Worth. I shot something like 78-70 and wasn't even close to making the cut. I'll never forget something he said to me that day.

I was playing the eighth hole of the Championship Course, a par-5. I had hit a good drive and wanted to hit my second shot with my Wilson 1200 3-wood. I asked Keith if I should hit the 3-wood, and what advantage would I have getting closer to the green, and he said, "What's the use, Robert, you don't know where the ball is going to go." No truer words could have been spoken.

I was determined to hit the 3-wood after hearing Keith's comment and I nailed the shot. I hit it very, very hard and it went very, very far. Unfortunately, the shot was about 50 yards off line to the left. After that embarrassing incident, I spent the next few weeks practicing with that one club, so I could show Keith I had some control over the 3-wood.

Keith and I played a lot of golf together in the late 1970s and early 1980s. He lived over in Arlington, and I'd drive over there a lot because Keith's wife, Leigh, used their family car to get to her job. That left Keith without any transportation. In those days, Keith was a good player and would-be golf professional who just couldn't quite get it all together. But he was able to get us on good golf courses every now and then. Seems he knew a lot of people and had a knack for getting us a tee time.

The good news about Keith Flatt is that he finally moved to Las Vegas, Nevada, and got a job as a head golf professional at a course called Los Prados. He's been out there probably eight or nine years now. Keith and I were able to do some catching up when the Senior PGA Tour stopped in Las Vegas in April.

One of the reasons I never attempted to play professional golf was because I watched Keith closely for many years. He would try to go through qualifying and line up financial backers and do all the things you're supposed to do. I saw his repeated failures and felt that my game was not superior to his to the extent that I would have had any success, either.

Although I ruled out professional golf, I did develop another goal. That was to become one of the best, and most respected, amateur golfers in the North Texas area. This was something I felt I could possibly achieve—and maintain for years to come. You might say this was my comfort level.

The mid-1970s was the period in my life when I was living off an allowance of $20 a week. Everything extra I made, or that Barbara made (she was working as a teacher's aide at our kids' grade school, and later became a teacher herself at West Creek Elementary), we put back for our kids and their activities. To conserve my allowance for golf, I subsisted mainly on a diet of soup. I'd take a can of soup (chicken noodle was a favorite), water it down a bit, and make it last as my lunch for a couple of days.

After awhile, I figured out how to save on soup money. On the way to work, I'd drive through my Uncle Pascal Landers' pecan orchard on Silver Creek Road and help cut down on the squirrel population. I'd shoot a squirrel (or sometimes a rabbit) and make that my daily meal. I'd take the animal to Mitchell's, skin it, and have Voncille, who worked as a sales clerk, boil it on the hot plate she kept in the break area. I've never been a picky eater, so I didn't mind the taste of squirrel, which wasn't so bad.

Freddie Stewart, who also worked at the store as a sales clerk, would tease me about eating "road kill" for lunch, but I didn't mind all the ribbing. Besides, I had money in my pocket that could go into golf.

I spent the first eight months of 1974 preparing for the Fort Worth City Championship. I was out there in January hitting the shots I knew I would need come Labor Day weekend. I developed a plan for which clubs to hit on which holes, where to miss the shots, which greens not to hit over, that sort of thing. Other guys might try to squeeze in four or five practice rounds at Pecan Valley in the weeks leading up to the tournament. But by then, I might have hit 10,000 balls practicing just the tee shot on the 16th hole.

Basically, in 1973, 1974 and 1975, I was hitting at least 70,000 shag balls a year and only playing 10 rounds of golf. That must sound pretty hard to believe, but it's true.

Despite all my practice and preparation, however, I didn't bring home the trophy. For the second straight year at Pecan Valley, I finished third. Bill Morrell won the tournament with a 217, and T.A. Avarello was runner-up at 218. I shot 220. I was knocking on the door to victory, but I couldn't keep from making too many costly mistakes. My course management was not what it should have been.

My big breakthrough in golf came in 1976, when I finally won the Fort Worth City Championship at Z. Boaz. I shot rounds of 73-72-68/213, or three-over. The crucial moment came at the par-4 on the 17th hole on the final day. I had just made a 10-foot putt for par at 16 to maintain a one-stroke lead over Ted McGee.

I used a 1-iron for the tee shot, and had 70 yards left to the pin, which was cut shallow and right, just behind a bunker. Because the other guys hit driver, I played first. I decided to aim 10 feet left of the pin and play to the middle of the green, beyond the hole. As it happened, I chose a sand wedge, hit the ball thin and not as far as I had planned.

The ball hit the upslope on the front of the green and kicked hard right, three feet from the pin. Neither of the other guys got close, and Ted wound up with a bogey. I made the birdie putt and coasted home on 18.

That was one of the happiest days in my life. It gave me a feeling of success a person doesn't get to experience too often. I also realized that in order for someone to find peace and comfort in an endeavor like golf, you must remain patient. For years, if necessary.

The evening before the final round, I hit about 300 balls with my 6-iron, swinging at about three-quarters strength. I believe this practice technique grooved my swing and gave me the timing needed to hit the ball close to the hole the next day. I've used that practice method ever since and recommend it. When there is a club championship or some big event on your golf calendar, tune up for it by hitting plenty of balls at a moderate pace. Don't hit a few balls—or a lot of balls—hard. You'll wreck your tempo.

My confidence was peaking in 1976. On July 22, I shot my lowest round ever, a 63 at Pecan Valley. I was playing that day with a regular golf buddy of mine named Hap Owens, who had won the Fort Worth Senior Men's Championship in 1974. I shot 30 on the front and came back in 33. My game was getting into a groove. I probably shot 10 or 11 consecutive rounds in the 60s, before I ever slipped back into the 70s.

That same summer, I entered the Texas State Open at Horseshoe Bay, near Marble Falls, for the first time. I drove down there a couple days ahead of time to get in some practice, and hooked up with Don Dodgen and Leroy Pearson, two really good players out of TCU.

Don Dodgen, who had won some mini-tour events in Texas and was the head golf professional at Singin' Hills in Fort Worth in the late 1970s, is one of the best players I've known. Somewhere around 1980, he got out of golf and into the oil business, and moved to Springtown, just up the Jacksboro Highway from Azle. Don's wife, Sue, and her daughters, Wendy and Kari, used to come into the Mitchell's store in Azle all the time. The girls were golfers, and I was always talking with them about their game.

Don Dodgen could hit a golf ball a country mile. When they started having all those long-driving contests back in the mid-1970s, I asked Don one day why he didn't enter them. I figured he could beat all the local guys in a breeze, me included. "It's simple," he answered. "Because I can't even beat him."

"Him" was Leroy Pearson, a long lanky guy from Eastland who took a shot at the mini-tours for awhile. Leroy could stand on the tee, crank up and hit the biggest ol' power fade you've ever seen. He probably carried the ball 260 yards or more, and with the hard fairways in West Texas, his drives always rolled well beyond 300 yards. That's large. If you want to read some funny stories about Leroy, who's a hilarious guy, check out *The Green Road Home* by Michael Bamberger. That's a great golf book.

A day before the 1976 Texas State Open started, Don and Leroy said they wanted to go visit a friend of theirs in San Marcos. They invited me to tag along. We drove down to San Marcos, which is between Austin and San Antonio, and on the way played a little golf course near Dripping Springs. After the round was over, we headed for a bar in San Marcos, and they sat around drinking beer and telling stories. Put Don and Leroy together, and you've got two characters out of a Dan Jenkins novel.

On the drive back to Horseshoe Bay, I said something about how poorly I'd played that day.

"Let's face it, Robert," drawled Leroy, who's one of the slowest talkers on the planet. "You're another has-been....just like the rest of us."

After watching me play that day, Don and Leroy weren't sure my game was ready for a tough layout like Horseshoe Bay. Funny thing, though, when the tournament started, I played pretty decent and made the cut of low 60 and ties. I wound up as the fourth lowest amateur. Those guys both missed the cut.

The next year, though, Don Dodgen nearly won the Texas State Open. He finished runner-up to Bobby Walzell from Houston. On the last day in 1977, Don was paired with Austin native and PGA Tour star Ben Crenshaw, and he became probably one of the only guys ever to see Crenshaw four-putt a green. That happened on the 17th hole, where Ben four-putted from 15 feet. Don said it wasn't a pretty sight. But since Ben Crenshaw's probably the best pure putter ever to come out of Texas, or anyplace else, you couldn't forget something like that.

I found at Horseshoe Bay that I had missed winning a trophy, which was given to the three low amateurs, by one spot. I immediately set myself a new goal: Come back to the Texas State Open and win one of those trophies.

MY CLOSING 66 BROUGHT ME IN AT 205, OR EIGHT-UNDER PAR.

In 1977, I tried to defend my Fort Worth City Championship at Pecan Valley, but fell a few shots short. I'm not sure why, but I never was able to repeat in the city tournament. And I never was able to win at Pecan Valley, period, even though I set the course record there, (with that 63, and shot a couple 64s, as well. But that's golf.

In 1978, though, I won the Fort Worth City Tournament for a second time. I was paired in the last group on the final day at Rockwood with Melvin Starks, who was leading the tournament, and Rod Trammell and Rudy Flores, who had won the Pan American National Championship two weeks earlier in Kansas City.

I came out blazing in the final round, shooting 31 on the front side. On the back side, I had three birdies and two bogeys, both of them three-putts. One had come at the 16th hole, when lightning flashed nearby. I hated seeing that. It makes me nervous.

My closing 66 brought me in at 205, or eight-under par, and in a tie with Starks, who was nicknamed Mousey. Mousey and I went into a sudden-death playoff that began on the first hole, a par-5. I hit a drive and three-iron to the front of the green and two-putted from

50 feet for birdie. Mousey was just short of the green in two shots, pitched to six feet and missed his birdie putt.

Winning the city tournament again at that particular time in my life was very important, because it gave me a winner's attitude and reassured me that all my hard work was worthwhile.

One of the best deals that ever happened to me in golf occurred that same year. I got a phone call from Pete Blessing, a nice fellow and good player, who said, "Hey, they're having trouble filling up the championship flight for the Diamond Oaks Fall-Out, the big tournament each fall at Diamond Oaks Country Club in Haltom City. Want to play with me?"

"Sure I do, Pete, " I replied. "I really do like that golf course."

Even though neither one of us was a member at Diamond Oaks, we went over there and played pretty decent the first two days. We were in good shape, near the lead. After the second round, I happened to ask Pete what kind of prizes we would be playing for the next day.

"I don't know," answered Pete. "Guns or something."

"Guns?" I hollered. "Did you say guns?"

I made a beeline to the pro shop and man, right there bigger than life, were the prizes. An Ithaca SKB 12 Gauge Automatic Shotgun, with a hardcase, was first prize. A lever-action 30-30 with a scope was second prize. A Black Hawk .357 was third prize.

I raced back to find my partner. "Pete, we can't lose in this deal," I said. "They've definitely got my full attention now."

We won the Diamond Oaks Fall-Out the next day, but not before a playoff. On the first sudden-death hole, I drove into the right trees, then hit a big slice with a 5-iron up on the green and sank a winning par putt. We took home the Ithaca shotguns, probably my favorite prize ever for winning a golf tournament.

We were a little lucky that day, to tell the truth. On the 17th hole, we're in contention, trying hard to win, and Pete hits a good drive in the fairway. So I try to lay up too close to the water, which cut through the fairway, only I hit it into the water. Now the pressure's on Pete. He hits a 4-iron to the green and half-shanks the shot. His ball flies out into the river, where it hits a big ol' cotton-wood tree and ricochets onto the green. He makes his par to keep our chances alive.

That's golf. Some days you get the breaks and things go your way. Other times, the breaks go against you and the golf gods smile on someone else. You just have to accept that, and get on with your business.

In 1978, my third appearance in the Texas State Open, I achieved a milestone of sorts. We were playing at Horseshoe Bay again, and I shot an opening 76. I followed that up with a 74, including a birdie on the final hole, my first birdie in two days. That was a real timely birdie, too, because the cut came at 150.

Later, I was checking the scoreboard and I saw that only three amateurs had made the cut. "Hot dog," I said, "I'm going to win one of those beautiful trophies." I was so jacked up, that in the final two rounds I shot 70-70, four-under par, and finished as the low amateur in the tournament.

That Texas State Open finish would rank as my biggest accomplishment in golf before 1980. In May 1980, I made it through two rounds of United States Open qualifying at Shady Valley in Arlington and earned a ticket to the big show. I think it helped a great deal that both rounds of qualifying, local and sectional, were scheduled for the same golf course. That gave me a chance to pick up some local knowledge and come up with a game plan.

In the first round of qualifying, I shot 147, seven-over par, and finished one stroke behind the low qualifier. Then in the second round, I shot 143, three-over, and got into a four-way sudden-death playoff for the final two spots.

I would have qualified without all the additional stress, if I had not made two double-bogeys on the final nine holes. As it was, I had to birdie my final hole, which was the ninth hole at Shady Valley, to make the playoff. I hit a good drive, a sand wedge to three feet and rolled in the putt to keep my chances alive.

The playoff foursome consisted of David Sann, a good player who had just graduated from TCU, Robert Hoyt, a pro who had been a collegiate standout at the University of Houston, and Arthur Russell, an American who played on the European Tour, and me, the manager of a Mitchell's Department Store.

We went back to the number one, a short par-4. We all hit good tee balls to within 50 or 60 yards of the green, but we all hit our little wedge shots over the putting surface. I guess everyone was having trouble controlling the adrenaline. Then three of us chipped up and one-putted for par, but Robert Hoyt failed to get up-and-down and was eliminated. Now we had three players for two spots.

Sann, Russell and I made par-5s at the second hole. On the third hole, a little par-3, I missed the green to the left and had to play an almost impossible chip. I did as well as I could have hoped for, running the ball 10 feet beyond the hole. The other guys made easy pars, but I had to sink that pressure putt coming back to stay in the hunt.

The fourth hole at Shady Valley is a straightaway par-4, with an out-of-bounds fence down the left side. David Sann, who was hitting ahead of me in the order, cranked his 1-iron tee shot over the fence. After I saw that, I played the hole as conservatively as possible, driving to the right, bunting my ball up near the green, chipping on and two-putting for a bogey 5. Russell made par but Sann, after that tee shot, could do no better than a double-bogey six. I was headed to the mother ship of American golf tournaments: the 80th United States Open.

Incidentally, in a practice round at Shady Valley before the U.S. qualifying, I made my first hole-in-one. I hit an eight-iron on the par-3 third hole, which can be anywhere from a five-iron to a nine-iron, depending on the wind. I remember I was playing with Dan Gray, a good player affiliated somehow or other with Texas Wesleyan College in Fort Worth.

I've since made one other hole-in-one, which came a couple years after that, in an Azle Golf Association tournament at Rockwood. I made an ace at the par-3 on the 16th hole, hitting a Kroydon pitching wedge. Funny, but that was the first time I ever swung that club. I found a Kroydon head and put it on a cheap shaft and stuck in the bag that day. The 16th hole is 120 yards and I thought, "Heck, I'll just use this club." I couldn't believe it when the ball headed straight for the stick and then disappeared. I kept that club for awhile, but finally sold it at a flea market. Incidentally, my dad, who witnessed the hole-in-one at Rockwood, has made three aces in his life. I hope to catch up with him one of these days soon.

In June 1980, Barbara and I and a friend of ours named Mike Deubler, whom she called Doo Doo and who was going to be my caddy, flew up to New Jersey for the U.S. Open at the famous Baltusrol Country Club. I figured that tournament would show me how my game stacked up against the best golfers in the world.

I was right, it did. I saw immediately that I was outmatched. I didn't have the shots, the ball flight or enough spin and control, to play with those guys. Not on that golf course, anyway.

Let me tell you, Baltusrol was one tough son of a gun. In the practice rounds, for example, I discovered that my drives only carried about 25 yards past beyond the point where they started mowing the fairways. That was not an especially encouraging sign.

The rough surrounding the fairways at Baltusrol looked to be about knee-high, and the greens were ten times faster than anything I'd ever encountered on the municipal courses around Fort Worth. There was so much slope in some of the greens, I had a couple chip shots where I couldn't even keep the ball on the putting surface. About the only thing that seemed halfway normal was the sand in the traps—although some of the traps were grass bunkers, which was something new to me.

Another thing was the fairways weren't mowed all the way to the green, meaning I couldn't hit run-up shots like you could back home. A player needed to hit high, soft shots with plenty of backspin to have any chance at all at Baltusrol. I was out of my element.

I shot 83 in the first round—a mere 20 strokes behind the co-leaders, Jack Nicklaus and Tom Weiskopf. Their opening 63s tied the U.S. Open scoring record for low 18 holes, which Johnny Miller had set during his celebrated final round at Oakmont in

1973. At least I didn't post the highest score in the field: someone named Barry Holt shot 85, and Russell Clark had 87.

As bad as that day was for me, it was even worse for my caddy. Doo Doo was so nervous that he started huffy and wheezing, and dang near hyperventilating, before every shot. I mean, he was so overcome by the experience, the large crowds and high-stakes atmosphere, that he was sucking for air. It was a pitiful sight.

Until he put on a caddy outfit and picked up my bag, Doo Doo looked like he could have been one of the competitors. Or I guess he looked more like a player than I. Right before we teed off, a USGA official, who was acting as starter, sized up my jeans, sneakers and Azle Golf Association cap and decided I must be the caddy. He walked over to Deubler and extended his hand. "Welcome to the United States Open, Mr. Landers," he said.

"I'm not Mister Landers," replied Doo Doo, pointing over at me. "He is Mister Landers." The starter was quick to apologize, but I could see where he might have been confused.

Fortunately, things went a little better for both of us in the second round. I shot 77, playing out of mind to shoot that low, and Doo Doo calmed down enough to breathe like a regular human being. Jack Nicklaus went on to win the 1980 U.S. Open, his fourth, after an exciting duel with Japan's Isao Aoki, while we went back to Fort Worth, bloodied but unbowed.

Galyn Wilkins wrote in the *Fort Worth Star-Telegram* that "Landers' first trip to an Open was what you might call a learning experience." He was right: I learned I was out of my league.

The most memorable part of my one and only trip to the U.S. Open came during the first practice round. When I got to the course on Monday afternoon, Andy Bean and George Burns were standing on the first tee getting ready to play.

I went up and introduced myself and asked if I could join them. Under other circumstances, I might have been too shy to take the initiative like that, but in golf I have a somewhat different personality. I feel pretty good about myself on a golf course, equal to the other guy, and I'm more assertive in golf than in other areas of my life. Besides, I figured the worst they could do was turn me down, in which case I could have simply waited and teed off after them.

But Bean and Burns were both real receptive and said, "Come on, let's go." So I played along with them, with a light rain falling. We went a few holes, then we caught up with Jerry Pate, the 1976 U.S. Open champion, who was playing by himself. We played a few more holes, then while we were standing on a tee, waiting for a fairway to clear, who walks up, but Raymond Floyd? So I got to play a hole with him, too.

Then it started raining harder, and since we were near the clubhouse, Bean, Pate and Floyd all decided to pack it in. George Burns told them, "You guys go ahead. I'm going to stay out here with Robert." Who knows, he might have just wanted to see more of the golf course, but I kind of had the feeling he might have stayed out there for my benefit, so I wouldn't have felt like the Lone Ranger.

George Burns treated me really well that day and made me feel welcome. I've never seen him again, or talked to him, but as long as I live, I'll never forget one thing he told me that day. He said, "No matter what anybody says, Robert, you've earned the right to be here. Just like the rest of us."

I very much appreciated hearing that from him. That's the same feeling I had in early 1995, when I started on the Senior PGA Tour. I felt like I had earned my rightful place inside the ropes. It certainly wasn't given to me.

I also got to play practice rounds at Baltusrol with Bob Gilder, who's still plugging away on the PGA Tour, and Pat Fitzsimons. They, too, were really nice and made me feel at ease.

Later that summer, I qualified for the 1980 U.S. Amateur Championship at the Country Club of North Carolina in the Pinehurst area. That's one of the prettiest places I have ever seen. I shot 76-76/152, barely missing the cut, which turned out to be a blessing. I was able to get back to Fort Worth in time for the city championship. Mike Deubler had sent in my entry form; maybe he knew somehow I would miss the cut in North Carolina.

By qualifying for the U.S. Open and the U.S. Amateur in 1980, I received an invitation to play in the 1981 Sunnehanna Amateur in Johnstown, Pennsylvania, which is one of the premier events in U.S. amateur golf. I mean, that's really fine stuff up there. I got to rub shoulders with some real top-flight amateurs, like Hal Sutton and Jodie Mudd.

What I needed more than all that shoulder rubbing, however, was finding someone who could rub my back. Seems that before I headed to Pennsylvania, I had to rearrange the store in Azle. We moved a lot of counters and displays, and I did a lot of heavy lifting. I was trying to get the job done real fast, so I could concentrate on the golf tournament.

I flew to Pennsylvania the next morning, and in the afternoon got in a practice round. The next day, when I tried to get out of bed, I couldn't. My back had frozen up on me, big time. It took me almost all day to stand up. Just sitting up was a difficult, painful process.

 Despite having a stiff lower back, I played pretty well in the Sunnehanna. The tournament didn't start until three days later, which gave me time to work out some of the kinks. As I recall, I tied for 19th place with Bob Lewis and Jay Sigel, who had been members of the United States' Walker Cup team. That's some pretty good company to keep.

After Sunnehanna, I rode up to New England with a guy named George Lucas, whom I had met at Baltusrol the previous year, and we played in the Vermont Open. But my back, probably aggravated by the long car ride, gave me fits the whole time. I played really poorly, and was ready to get back to Texas.

The back problems that surfaced on that trip to the eastern United States in 1981 set the tone for what was ahead: scaling back my competitive phase in golf. I played for another year or so, though never quite as well as before. When the back pain wouldn't go away, and finally started getting worse, I put down my sticks and decided to get on with my life.

Chapter Seven

GOLF TAKES A
BACK SEAT

My golf career, such as it was, came to a crossroads in the early 1980s. The back pain I experienced beginning at the Sunnehanna Amateur in Pennsylvania in 1981 slowed things down and forced me to stop playing competitive golf.

Actually, the first time I can remember hurting my back was somewhere around 1969, in the jet shop at Carswell AFB. We were trying to put a turbine wheel on a jet engine. Those wheels weighed about 125 pounds or so, and took two people to handle because of the sharp edges. There were seven bolts in the shaft that you had to slide the wheel on, and one of the bolts was offset. Alignment was a problem, because you didn't know which exact bolt, unless you had marked the wheel when you took it off.

In this case, we were working with a new turbine wheel, and the tolerances were so small it was almost impossible to tell where the offset was. It was mostly a trial-and-error process, and if you were wrong, you'd have to try it and turn it, try it and turn it. We had to do a bunch of turning on this one wheel, and we were bent over because the stand you put the wheel on was about knee-high. By the time we got the wheel on right, I knew I'd hurt my back.

I got over that pretty quickly, but as time went on, I began having a little back trouble every now and then. Who knows, maybe the wear-and-tear of hitting so many golf balls for so many years had something to do with it. Or the fact that I didn't get any real exercise to speak of, other than hitting golf balls—which should not be confused with walking, jogging, lifting weights or any kind of real workout. Also adding to the pressure on my back was the fact that I had to stand on my feet, for long periods every day, on the concrete floor at Mitchell's.

Anyway, by the early 1980s, my golf game started heading south. I remember trying to qualify for the U.S. Open in 1983 at Diamond Oaks, and narrowly missing. My son, Robert III, was caddying that day, and we were even par for the day on our 35th hole, the par-4 17th, the same hole where Pete Blessing bounced that shot off the tree when we won the Diamond Oaks Fall-Out.

I had hit a 1-iron into the middle of the fairway and had a 5-iron to the green. The shot was about 165 yards into a 10-mph wind, and I planned to hit a low punch shot under the wind and into the middle of the green.

When I swung that 5-iron, though, I laid the sod over the ball. I hit that sucker so fat that the ball barely made it to the middle of the river. When Robert, who was sunburned, had blisters on his feet and was exhausted from lugging my big bag all day, saw my ball disappear with a splash, he fell down in the fairway, my golf club on top of him.

"That's it," he said. "I'm not taking another step."

I understood completely. "You go on, Rob," I told him. "I'll tote my bag in. It's no big deal."

Robert got up and headed straight for the parking lot at Diamond Oaks and drove away. After making double bogey on 17 and par on 18, I finished two-over and missed by one shot being an alternate.

That was the only time my son ever carried my golf bag for me, and I don't blame him a bit for not coming back. Still, we've shared many good times together on the golf course. When he was a little fellow, I made some cut-down clubs for him, and I'd take him over to Rockwood Park and we'd hit balls together.

Golf gave us extra time together. During the years, my son played a lot of golf with me and my dad, and he would also play in Azle Golf Association tournaments. Rob worked for awhile at the Pecan Valley and Z. Boaz courses, and the Benbrook driving range. He played golf in high school, at Western Hills H.S., before injuring his knee in an auto accident. After he started college, though, he was always too busy hitting the books, or being involved with other activities, to have much time for golf.

Rob and I hunted and fished together even more than we played golf. We'd go duck hunting, deer hunting, quail hunting, you name it. One of his favorite stories is about the time I shot an 11-point buck with his .22 Hornet, up at Poolville. I have that trophy mounted in our living room. From his earliest years, we also did a lot of fishing for catfish or perch. Sometimes, Phil Henderson and I would take Rob with us down to the Brazos River. Other times, I'd take Rob and some of his friends, like Drew Humphries, to the lake or the creeks. I must have passed a lot of my love for the outdoors on to Rob, because he's a lot like me in that respect.

*

ROBERT GOT UP AND HEADED STRAIGHT FOR THE PARKING LOT AT DIAMOND OAKS AND DROVE AWAY.

I also recall trying to qualify for the U.S. Open at Diamond Oaks on one other memorable occasion, in 1982. We were playing in threesomes that day, and our group was going off the 10th tee. One of my playing partners was supposed to be Johnny Elliott's son. Johnny was a friend, who owned a golf club repair shop across the highway from Rockwood Municipal.

Guess what? The Elliott kid didn't show up, leaving us with a twosome. I was standing on the tee, all ready to go, when my playing partner, whose name I can't remember, went into a panic because he was missing his 7-iron. Seems he'd left the club leaning against the Diamond Oaks clubhouse. He went running off to retrieve it, and by the time he got back to the tee, USGA official

Frank Anglim was steaming. We were already late, and we were about to hold up play even more.

I was playing that day with one of my most treasured golf possessions, a Sandy Auchterlonie brassie (2-wood) made in 1924. I had changed the brassie from 14 degrees to 11 degrees, and added an insert with a 43" shaft. This club, a genuine classic, has a very shallow face with a large deep head. Normally, I hit that club really well, but on that day I caught my first tee shot in the heel, and the ball shot straight left, into the river. Then my playing partner steps up and he hits one in the water. By the time we finished the hole, we were 15 minutes behind. Frank was fuming.

On the par-3 12th hole, I got up-and-down from the greenside bunker for par. After I finished, my playing partner, who had a three-footer left for par, forgot where he was and what he was doing. He just spaced out. He put the flag in the cup and started to head for the next tee.

Being the sort of helpful and concerned opponent I always try to be, I suggested that the guy might want to finish the hole. Frank Anglim was sitting in a golf cart behind the green watching this exchange. As the fellow putted out, Frank politely told me that if I had only kept my mouth shut, and let the guy tee off on the next hole, my opponent would have been disqualified. That would have solved some of Frank's problems with slow play.

As it was, we were probably the slowest twosome in the history of local qualifying for a U.S. Open. This guy shot rounds of 89-92—and he was supposed to be either a 2-handicap (or better) amateur or a qualified professional. I don't recall my scores, but after that opening drive, I didn't take much time before I hit. I did spend most of the day, however, helping that poor guy try to find his golf ball. I think Frank Anglim, to this day, still owes me a decent pairing for having to put up with that.

By 1983, I stopped playing golf as much, or as hard, as I had before. I didn't quit the game altogether, but I stopped entering the Fort Worth City Championship or attempting to qualify for the U.S. Amateur or U.S. Open. I would still hit golf balls every now and

then, and I played an occasional round with friends or family, but I
didn't devote my full attention to the game. I didn't put in all the
long hours of work.

The primary reason for this change in the program was that
my lower back was killing me. I couldn't swing a golf club without
feeling pain. I couldn't walk without discomfort. I couldn't bend
down to tie my shoelaces or lift any heavy objects. My left leg was
going numb.

The source of all the pain was a pinched sciatic nerve. Over
the next three years, I went to see three separate chiropractors, a
Doctor Johnson in Arlington and Doctors Schultz and Masson in
Azle, for treatment. With each one, it was the same deal: My back
would feel decent for about six months, then I'd need treatment for
the next six months.

When all was said and done, I ended up out on Freddie
Stewart's farm, doing a lot of hard, physical labor, which got me in
decent shape and must have strengthened my back muscles. The
back pain went away and since that time—knock on wood—I
haven't had any more trouble.

How I got out to the farm in the first place requires a bit of
explanation.

In the summer of 1985, Freddie Stewart's husband, Bill, asked
her for a divorce. She was very upset, naturally, and she shared her
pain and feelings of rejection with me. I tried to offer what comfort
and consolation I could.

By this time, Freddie had become my assistant manager at
Mitchell's and we were very close friends and confidants. We'd been
working together for more than 11 years, during which time we had
developed a special bond. I can remember cutting firewood and taking it to the Stewarts' house in the winter so Freddie could enjoy
some fires. Her husband wouldn't cut wood, or buy any, so I decided to give them some.

I had come to look upon Freddie as a special person, somebody who was a really good friend. I admired her common sense
about things. She could offer answers, or guidance, on questions I

would have about running the store. Or anything else. She had a real level head, and sincerity and honesty in everything she did. When problems came up, Freddie would always try to do the right thing.

She also had the ability to help analyze all the facts needed to make a good decision. Freddie's decisions always made a lot of sense to me. And if she felt strongly about something she had decided, she would stick to her guns. She wasn't about to change her mind if she thought she was right. I admired her strength and ability to do the right thing—regardless of what anyone else thought. She never played politics or put up with any of that stuff.

What Freddie didn't know, and what I was tormenting myself trying to find a way to tell her, was that by the time her husband asked her for a divorce, my own marriage had hit the skids.

It was like Barbara had her life and I had my life, and they didn't overlap much. As our kids got older and got away from home (Robert III had gone off to college in Austin by then, and Barbee was finishing up high school and getting ready to go to Tarrant County Junior College), the significance of our lives together as a couple was a lot less than before. We both had come to the realization we had hardly anything in common.

Barbara didn't like to do any of the things I liked, golf included. For example, she resented the fact I spent $400 on a set of golf clubs in 1974, and I don't think she ever forgave me for that until I took her to the U.S. Open in 1980. At that point, she could see that the money had been a good investment, but until then it was like I had wasted $400, and she had been holding a grudge.

Barbara hated hunting and fishing, too. She didn't like guns at all, and she didn't want me buying them or fooling with them. When I'd come home from fishing, she'd wrinkle up her nose and tell me I smelled all fishy.

On the other hand, I didn't want to do things she wanted to do, especially when it came to entertainment and social-type stuff. I was never willing to leave home, for example, unless I was going to play in a golf tournament somewhere. Barbara enjoyed things like going somewhere just to sightsee, or going on a vacation. To me, that was kind of like wasting time and not having any benefit from what it costs you to do those things.

I never did have the money to do things I wanted to do, like play in golf tournaments, and I certainly wasn't going to spend any money on something I knew I wasn't going to enjoy.

Sometime late in 1985, several months after the Stewarts had separated, I wrote Freddie a letter that expressed my deepest feelings. All the emotions building inside me, all the guilt I had about being married to one woman and being in love with another, came spewing out, like a gusher in an oilfield.

I told Freddie I loved her. I told her I had a fear of dying, or of something terrible happening to one of us, before I could ever tell her how I truly felt.

I let her know that she had been in my fantasies for a long time. I said that my feelings for her were a burden I had carried with me for years. I told her I compensated by pouring my energies into golf, and that I had worked on my game the hardest and played my best when I was at my lowest emotional and mental level. Now that I wasn't playing any competitive golf, I had no such outlet. I was losing sleep at night, and in a constant state of worry.

"I can't cope with my feelings any more," I wrote. "It is like a yo-yo up and down. I can be feeling good one minute and the next, as fast as one breath later, I have a flash and I will be crying, especially when I am by myself.

I gave Freddie the letter, written on lined yellow paper from a legal pad, at the end of work one day. I'm sure the letter must have caught Freddie off-guard. She probably had never thought of me as anything more than her boss or her friend. Now here I was, coming on to her. Coming on strong.

The next day, after the store closed, we stayed late and had a heart-to-heart talk. We talked over our feelings, bared our souls, and admitted that both our marriages were lacking in certain respects. We did agree, however, they were better marriages than a lot of others we could name.

I knew after that conversation Freddie wasn't irritated with me. She could have told me to get lost, or to just forget it. I had taken a big risk by giving her the letter, because she might have told me to get out of her life completely, and that was the last thing I wanted.

"I know I am wrong for some of the things I want to say, especially to you," I had written in the letter. "You may hate me for it. I may even run you off. I hope not, because I need to let it out. I am very sorry I am to the point of doing this, please try to forgive me. I can control my physical actions much better than I can my mental ones. Anything less than what I want to say would not be truthful."

Freddie had finally heard the truth from me—how deeply I cared about her—and she didn't seem to mind.

Not long after I gave her the letter, Freddie and I started seeing each other outside of work, on a real low-profile basis. We would drive up to Poolville to fish in the tank on my dad's property, the farm where Winnie was lost and later found. Every now and then, we would hit a few golf balls at the Circle T Driving Range (now Casino Beach Golf Academy), and once we played miniature golf over in Lake Worth. Mostly, though, we did things that didn't cost any money. We just hung out with each other, talking up a blue streak and enjoying being together.

I remember that on my 42nd birthday, on Jan. 6, 1986, we drove down to Crawford, Texas, near Waco, and visited the town where Freddie was born and raised. That was a special trip for me, because I wanted to learn all about her. I knew I wanted to devote my life to her.

Our feelings toward each other intensified over the next year. We continued to be together 12 hours a day at Mitchell's, and we would spend time alone every now and then. One time, I took my trumpet down to the store and played "Secret Love," the Doris Day standard that was one of my favorites. I thought I was being pretty cute and charming, but Freddie told me later it was pretty transparent. As usual, she was probably right.

FREDDIE HAD FINALLY HEARD THE TRUTH FROM ME— HOW DEEPLY I CARED ABOUT HER— AND SHE DIDN'T SEEM TO MIND.

We knew our relationship wasn't the sort of thing we could keep hidden forever from the other Mitchell's employees. We also knew that the company wasn't too keen about employees getting involved, or any of that sort of stuff.

In November 1986, Freddie had the chance to go to work at a dress shop on Main Street in Azle, owned by a woman named Liz Hutchison. It's probably a good thing Freddie had that choice, because our relationship, sooner or later, would have created problems for us at Mitchell's and may have even jeopardized our jobs.

I remember telling Freddie when she left Mitchell's that my most sincere wish was that some day we would have the opportunity to work together, or be together, and not have to go our separate ways to work. I'm not sure if I thought maybe one day I'd have my own business, or something like that. I just wanted her to know that I wanted to be with her all the time. Being on the 1995 Senior PGA Tour gives us that chance. It's probably the best part of the whole deal.

In January 1987, I moved out on Barbara and moved in with Freddie at her house on the farm. Freddie's divorce from Bill wasn't yet final—the lawyers were having trouble working things out and dividing their property, which included the farm—but we had reached the point where we couldn't stand to live apart any longer.

You see, Freddie and I have a special bond, an understanding about the way the other one thinks and feels. We have respect for each other and accept our differences. We're on our own special wavelength. If people really do have soul mates, then Freddie is mine.

Freddie's family wasn't too overjoyed to learn I had moved to the farm. Her grown daughters, Lisa and Vicky, had a lot of mixed feelings about the situation. One day, they'd be happy their mother had a new man in her life, a man who put her on a pedestal and treated her like a queen. The next day, they would wonder why Freddie was being so cruel to their father.

Barbara and I never really had any quarrel about my leaving. Looking back, she was probably glad to see me go. My kids never said a negative thing to me about it, either. They might have felt differently, or held a grudge against me, had Barbara been upset. But she wasn't and, as a result, neither were they.

Bill Stewart, on the other hand, wasn't too thrilled with these developments. I half-expected him to get a gun and come looking to shoot me. But we never had a confrontation of any kind. It's like I'd made a choice, right or wrong, to be with Freddie. I was going to stick with that choice, no matter what.

I didn't leave Barbara or the kids high and dry. I continued to pay the house mortgage and help out with the family bills. I continued to help pay for my kids' schooling. Just because I'd deserted the house didn't mean I would desert my responsibilities as their father.

I'd been living with Freddie on the farm for about six months, when in July 1987 the house burned down. I was at work at Mitchell's when Freddie called with the news. I went and picked her up at the dress shop and drove her out to the farm.

By the time the volunteer fire department from La Junta had arrived, the wood-frame house had pretty much gone up in smoke. Both of us lost most of our possessions. About all we had left were the clothes we wore to work that day. I poked around in the rubble and fished out a few burned golf clubs, a set of Mag Force irons, which I wound up playing with for years afterward.

One golf club that perished in the fire was a driver I'd made for Freddie when we first started dating. I had engraved the metal plate on the bottom of the club with Freddie's name. The driver was a beautiful blonde persimmon wood, which I built completely by hand, using a hacksaw and file to inlay the insert and soleplate.

I lost much of my gun collection in the fire, a total of something like 26 guns. All told, I probably lost 100 or more golf clubs. Another victim of the fire was my golf cart, an old clunker that, just like the bunny with batteries, kept going and going. My friend Ronnie Feemster likes to tell the story about the time we took the cart to a tournament in Decatur.

I didn't have a trailer, so I transported the cart in the bed of my pickup truck. The cart had been spray-painted a chocolate brown and its exterior had a bunch of tiny dents, the result of hail damage. It was missing a top, the Naugahyde seat covers were torn with the padding coming out, and one of the bag straps was missing. I had tied on a piece of cotton rope to hold in the passenger-side golf bag. Oh yes, the brakes didn't work, either.

Ronnie says that when I drove that cart up to the first tee, and then stepped out wearing my sneakers, the other guys looked at us like we were two of the original country bumpkins. They were making wisecracks about the cart, and my shoes, until I hit my first drive. Then all the talking stopped.

As Freddie and I came to realize, things like golf clubs and golf carts and guns are just material things. They can all be replaced. We were safe and unharmed, and that was the only thing that truly mattered. We figured that we could get along fine—as long as we had each other.

For the first few nights after the fire, we slept in a pick-up camper shell and bathed in a cow trough. Then we went out and bought a 36-foot travel trailer, which would become our home for the next three years.

The trailer had a little living room area with a couch, a little kitchen, a little bathroom and a little bedroom. Everything in a trailer home seems little. The closet space was limited, of course, but then we didn't have many clothes to put in them at first. We ended up having a bed specially made to replace the couch and lived in the front of the trailer. We used the bedroom as storage space.

> **WHEN I DROVE THAT CART UP TO THE FIRST TEE, AND THEN STEPPED OUT WEARING MY SNEAKERS, THE OTHER GUYS LOOKED AT US LIKE WE WERE COUNTRY BUMPKINS.**

In November 1987, Barbara and I ended our 22-year marriage. She called me one day and said, "Hey, don't you think it's time for us to get a divorce?"

"Yeah, if you want to, that's fine," I said. "No problem."

"Well, meet me down at Kenneth's," she said. Kenneth Price, an attorney, was a mutual friend of ours in Azle. We met outside his office and quickly went over how to split things up. Kenneth handled all the paperwork.

Barbara kept her savings from her job, and I kept mine from Mitchell's. She kept our bigger house in Benbrook, and everything that went with it, and I kept the little house we owned in River Oaks, which we were renting to her Aunt Elizabeth. That didn't help me too much, though, because we were renting the house for the family rate of $100 a month, which covered the house payment but was about three times less than the market rate. I later sold that house to my uncle, Tom McDaniel, and used the money to help with the down payment on the new house Freddie and I started building in 1990.

That's about the time we decided to get married. We were committed to each other—with or without a marriage license—but we talked it over and decided we should officially become husband and wife. We were planning on going to see a Justice of the Peace, but Steve Henton invited us to have the ceremony in his house, and we accepted.

As I mentioned earlier, Freddie and I were married on March 9, 1990. A friend of ours, Jeanette Smith, who worked for me at Mitchell's, was the witness. The mixed feelings within our families right about then were a little too high to ask anyone else to attend. We didn't want to make anyone feel uncomfortable. After the wedding ceremony, Freddie and I celebrated by going to dinner at Long John Silver's. We asked Jeanette to go along.

About the same time as our wedding, Tommy Spurrier, a contractor, poured the foundation for a new two-bedroom house on the farm. He brought his two boys, Clint and Joe, down to the farm and let them swim in the creek. I remember building a fire by the creek so the boys could warm up quickly after they came out of the water. It was March, and the water was cold.

The house was located about a half-mile or so from where the burned-down house had stood. I don't think Bill Stewart was too excited to hear the news that we'd gotten married, or that we were building a new house. He might have still felt, or wished, that one day Freddie would come back to him. They were married 35 years.

Not long after that, Bill took a fishing trip down to Three Rivers in South Texas. While he was down there, he suffered a serious heart attack. I drove Freddie down to South Texas so she could help her daughters, Vicky and Lisa, keep a vigil with him at the hospital in Beeville.

Bill never recovered. He died on April 18, 1990. He's buried in the little Bud Clark Cemetery that's on our property, next to their son, Randy, who was killed in a automobile accident in Azle in March 1978, and their infant grandchild, Michael Stewart Hall, who died of sudden infant death syndrome in May 1979.

Freddie and I moved into our new home in July 1990. We spent about $78,000 for the house, paying about $20,000 cash down and financing the rest through Azle State Bank. We bought new furniture and furnishings, paying cash for everything because neither of us likes to have any debt. Our goal was to pay off the house in seven years, by 1997. You can do that if you live real cheaply and don't spend any money on things like new cars, or vacations, or new farm equipment.

We currently owe $12,000 on the house, and as soon as we get all these new endorsement deals lined up, and can see where all our money really is, the first thing we want to do is pay off the house. That's for sure!

About the only competitive golf I played between 1983 and 1991—I don't consider the small-town tournaments on the Texas Barbecue Circuit anything more than fun golf—was the Oklahoma Open in 1987. Freddie and I decided to take a little trip to Colorado for a vacation that September, after we had gotten the Labor Day weekend sale at Mitchell's and all the big back-to-school rush behind us. It was only six weeks or so after the house fire, and with all the stress we'd been through, we felt we needed a break.

I had never been on a real vacation in my life, so I was looking forward to seeing Colorado, especially the mountains. Only I made one suggestion to Freddie: On the way to Colorado, we should swing by Oklahoma City, so I could play in the qualifying round for one of my favorite tournaments, the Oklahoma Open.

That way, I could get in a little golf on a real top-notch golf course, Oak Tree.

We drove up to Oklahoma City and stayed in the suburb of Edmond, where Oak Tree is located. Wouldn't you know it, I caught fire—maybe because I was using my burned golf clubs—and started playing really well. On the 14th hole, I had a 9-iron approach shot to the green, and my ball hit the bank about 15 feet above the flagstick and spun backward into the hole for an eagle two.

I finished with a 69 that day, which earned me a spot in the Oklahoma Open, competing against all those "Oak Tree Boys" like Bob Tway, Gil Morgan, David Edwards, Doug Tewell, Willie Wood and Scott Verplank. Rather than go on to Colorado, Freddie and I stayed around Edmond for the next few days while I played in the tournament. I didn't play very well, but I sure enjoyed being in competition again after such a long layoff.

As it stands, I still have never been to Colorado. If the Senior PGA Tour schedules a tournament up in Denver or Durango one of these days, maybe I'll get there yet.

And, who knows, maybe one day I'll take a real vacation.

Chapter Eight

MR. AND MRS. GREEN JEANS

Beginning in 1988, Freddie and I began raising cattle. We bought five little Holstein calves, two boys and three girls, when they were three days old. We named the boys Rocky and Dino, and the girls Daisy, Spooky and Hope. We gave Hope that particular name because she was real sick, and we hoped she would live.

Actually, Freddie comes up with most of the cows' names. She's pretty good with picking out descriptive ones. Franz Lidz wrote in his *Sports Illustrated* story that Freddie can think up names "faster than a bad-check artist."

All the calves were sickly, and little Rocky didn't survive. But Hope and the three others did. We bottle-fed the new members of our family for the first three months, giving them shots, Pepto-Bismal and pills from the feed store. We tried our best to nurse them back to health, and were pretty successful.

Once, when the calves were about six months old, Dino slipped off a 15-foot cliff and on to a little patch of creek bank near a bend in Ash Creek. Freddie and I tried to coax him back up the steep slope, but to no avail. He wouldn't come back up and he wouldn't go across the water, where the bank wasn't as steep. We stayed out with him until sundown, then left him there for the night.

The next morning, I got out our big tractor with the front-end loader and went to rescue Dino. I started cutting a notch at the top of the cliff, where Dino had fallen, and began pushing down the dirt to form a little ramp that Dino could climb up. He saw the sunlight coming through the notch I'd carved and up he came, rejoining our little herd.

Through the years, I've used that front-end loader to build and rebuild our creek crossing more times than I care to remember. The road usually lasts until a few "gully-washers," or hard rains, in the spring get the creek running at full throttle. That generally washes out the road, and I have to start all over.

Whenever we had a little extra money, we would buy more baby calves, which cost about $100 or $125, or weaned calves, which sell for $300 or $400 apiece, depending on the breed and weight. Our strategy was to keep the girls and sell the boys, including Dino.

When Daisy, Spooky and Hope reached about 15 months, we bought our first bull, which we named Soupy. After Soupy, a big old red Brangus bull, had been hanging around the farm for awhile, we had our first baby calves. Each was a girl, and we named them Cookie, CoCo and Gypsy.

Being Holsteins, the cows produced too much milk for the little calves, so Freddie and I had to learn how to milk them, something that neither of us had ever done. Since we enjoy doing things together so much, Freddie would get on one side of the cow and I would get on the other and we'd work together. We were pretty slow at milking, if you want to know the truth. Not like my Granny Landers, whom I can remember seeing in a real rhythm with her cows, filling milk pails in no time at all. Later, Freddie and I bought more calves to handle all the excess milk the mothers were producing.

Daisy and Spooky are still with our family, which now numbers close to 50 head. Hope got sick after her second calf, and we sold her. Gypsy was a jumping cow, so we sold her, too. After I lost my job at Mitchell's in 1992, and money got real tight, we decided we'd have to turn some of our calves into steak or ground round. We'd usually pick out the meanest and orneriest calf and take it to the slaughterhouse. Most of them have tasted about like their dispositions, a little tough. Now that we've improved our household finances, we'll probably go back to eating someone else's beef.

Freddie and I can recite all the names of the mother cows, which gets a little tricky now that the herd has grown so much. The bull's name is easy to remember—Gentle Ben, just like Ben Crenshaw's nickname. One of the hardest parts about being away on the golf tour in 1995 will be not getting to see our young calves growing up and our new calves being born.

Cattle are like children, in a way. They each have their own personalities and temperaments. They may look the same to an outsider, but each has distinguishing features, just like people. I like to show affection by petting them on their flanks, rubbing their faces and pulling on their horns. I also like to call them by name and watch them respond. Which, if it's near dinner time, they'll do. And which, if we're trying to get them in a pen or somewhere they don't want to go, they hardly do at all.

We don't make any money to speak of with our cattle. It's more like a break-even proposition. By the time we pay for feeding and caring, it's probably just a little bit better than a push. We try to use cattle money to pay our income taxes and that's it. But the cows add so much to our lives that I don't think Freddie and I could be completely happy without them.

Over the past seven years, I have either built or rebuilt all the fences, pens, sheds and gates on our property. It's been a very time-consuming process. But I'm not the sort to hire anyone to help me do what I can do myself.

Fences can be pretty expensive propositions, because the cows have the capacity to inflict plenty of damage to them with very little effort. Since I've made the Senior PGA Tour and made

> *
> THE BULL'S NAME IS
> EASY TO REMEBER—
> GENTLE BEN,
> JUST LIKE BEN
> CRENSHAW'S
> NICKNAME.

some money, we've been upgrading the fences on the farm with cedar stays. They make a big difference.

Some of the sheds are made from scrap materials other people threw away. After Mitchell's closed in 1992, I earned a little extra money by cleaning up people's yards. In addition to paying me a few dollars, some people allowed me to haul off pieces of wood, tin or metal. I could generally find some use for those materials on our farm, or I'd resell them.

Freddie especially enjoys plowing the fields, or mowing them down. Our tractor is a worn out 1940s model Minneapolis Moline, which is on its last legs. This spring, we've been having trouble getting the darn thing started. I thought it probably just needed a new starter switch, but we replaced the switch and the engine still wouldn't fire. If I knew what was wrong, I'd fix it.

We spend almost as much time trying to get the tractor to run as we do operating it. One of the things I hope to do with some of my winnings in professional golf is get us a new one. I went over to Weatherford the other day and looked at some John Deere tractors. And Jerry Hamilton has had a conversation with some Massey-Ferguson people about an endorsement arrangement in exchange for some farm equipment. I don't know if we'll get anything worked out, but I do know we need to upgrade our equipment.

Freddie just loves cows, and our house reflects that fact. We have a cow mailbox and cow cutouts in the yard (which photographers love to get into the pictures of me hitting balls). We have all kinds of cow knickknacks in the house—cow clocks, cow shelves, cow plates, cow this and that. Some we bought at flea markets or garage sales. Some we made ourselves.

I've also built Freddie a lot of bird houses, which she also likes. I've built them out of wood, in the shape of everything from cows and cactus, to armadillos and horses, to the state of Texas.

I've also built most of the roads on our farm. I'd shovel sand and gravel from the creek bed, using my front-end loader, and fill up the washed-out places. I'd haul up large rocks from the creek and use them to fill holes or low spots.

I have never disliked the physical labor associated with life on the farm. All the building and mending of fences, the clearing of brush, the chopping of wood.

Looking back, I'd have to say chopping firewood, probably as much as anything else, helped me resurrect my golf game. It takes plenty of hand-eye coordination to drive a sledgehammer into a wedge to split a log. It takes the same hand-eye coordination to swing an axe and deliver a clean, penetrating blow.

Swinging axes and sledgehammers strengthened my wrists, forearms, shoulders and back—all of which are pretty important in the golf swing. The swinging motion itself, although on a different plane than a golf swing, helped me practice delivering a powerful blow to a stationary object. Just as you do hitting a golf ball.

In my opinion, golfers can realize a big benefit from swinging a weighted club, and they sure can't hurt themselves any by swinging a sledgehammer or axe. You'll be working many of the large muscles used in the golf swing.

I can remember going to bed after a long day of splitting wood feeling sore from head to foot. Like the saying goes, "No pain, no gain." What I was gaining from all the wood cutting was strength and endurance, which helped me when I got back into golf. Hitting 300 or 400 golf balls a day, or sometimes as many as 500, is nothing compared with splitting a cord of wood.

One thing I enjoy most about farm life is you can stay busy all the time. Of course, I have never been one to sit around much, whether to watch TV or read a book or magazine. Occasionally, I'll go down to Dollar Bill's convenience store and rent a movie, partly because Bill only charges $1 for videos. As a rule, I'd rather be busy, and on the farm you can work all day, and most of the night. By the next day, there's always something else to do. Seems like you never quite catch up with all the chores.

That's not discouraging, though, because you can look around the place and see the results of your efforts. I'm one of those people who takes pride in seeing what I've accomplished. I feel that way about the work I've done on the farm, as well as the work I've done in golf. I may do things the hard way from time to time, but the satisfaction I've felt—mostly in a mental sense, not a financial sense—has been well worth the effort.

One time, for example, I had to put out some Bermuda seed after Freddie had just plowed the field. We didn't have anything to dispense the seed with, so I walked around our pastures using a little hand-held sower strapped around my neck. I seeded a total of 25 acres, and don't think that didn't take a lot of walking back and forth. After an experience like that, walking 18 holes on a golf course—or 72 holes in a tournament—is like hardly taking any steps at all. I was certainly proud to see that grass start to grow.

Besides cattle, we've always had a farm dog. Due to bad luck and misfortune, we've gone through several of them. When I moved in with Freddie in January 1987, we got a little dog named Tommy, a white spitz. The weekend before the house burned down that July, Tommy disappeared. A lot of things can happen to a dog in the country, of course, so disappearing is by no means unusual. That stuff happens.

A few weeks after that, a friend of mine at Mitchell's, Robin Weineke, gave me a little dog named Wee Willie The Fire Chief. Willie, a little-bitty brown dachsund that wasn't much bigger than a rat, was a great companion. He was with us for about a year, before meeting a terrible fate.

One night in the summer of 1988, there was a full moon. Not being the type to sit around, I decided to do some night mowing in one of the fields. I put gas in the tractor and wrapped a flashlight around the front to give me some additional light.

I cranked up the tractor, and the PTO, which activates the mower unit, was in gear. Somehow or other, Willie was under the mower blades at that very moment. The blade turned, and poor Willie met a sudden, swift death.

That episode nearly broke my heart. We buried Willie the next morning in a pretty little spot near a grove of trees. We call it Willie's Corner.

ROBERT, PRACTICING AS HE DID DAILY ON HIS FARM, IN FRONT OF THE ORIGINAL "MOO CREW".

FREDDIE AND ROBERT DOING THEIR BEST "AMERICAN GOTHIC" IMPERSONATION.

**TAKING A BREAK ON THE PRACTICE GREEN,
ROBERT SOAKS IN HIS FIRST SEASON ON THE PGA TOUR.**

**ROBERT ENJOYING THE ATTENTION OF THE NATIONAL MEDIA
AFTER HIS FIRST ROUND AS A TOURING PRO.**

FREDDIE CHATTING WITH DICK SCHAAP IN ONE OF
HER FIRST INTERVIEWS WITH THE NATIONAL PRESS.

ROBERT'S NEW HIGH PROFILE REQUIRES A LITTLE GETTING USED TO AT
NEWS CONFERENCES FOLLOWING EACH ROUND.

**ROBERT COILS TO HIT ONE OF HIS LONGEST
DRIVES OF THE DAY...HOLY COW!**

ROBERT TIPS HIS HAT TO THE GALLERY AFTER SINKING A TESTY 5-FOOTER TO SAVE PAR.

WITH SAND TRAPS GUARDING EVERY APPROACH SHOT, ROBERT SOON REALIZED HOW IMPORTANT HIS HOURS OF PRACTICE WITH HIS SAND WEDGE WOULD BE ON THE TOUR.

**ROBERT, IN HIS SIGNATURE TENNIS SHOES,
WATCHES A SHOT SAIL TO THE GREEN.**

**ROBERT APPRECIATES THE OPPORTUNITY TO STOP AND SIGN
AUTOGRAPHS FOR ALL HIS NEW FOUND FANS.**

ROBERT ADJUSTING TO THE FAST, DIFFICULT GREENS AT NAPLES.

ROBERT SAVING PAR WITH A CLASSIC UP AND DOWN.

ROBERT PREPARING TO HIT HIS SECOND SHOT TO THE GREEN ON ONE OF THE MONSTER PAR 5'S AT THE ROYAL CARIBBEAN.

ROBERT AND FREDDIE ENJOYING THE SPREAD IN THE PLAYERS TENT.

ALWAYS BY HIS SIDE, FREDDIE IS A CONSTANT SOURCE OF SUPPORT AND STRENGTH.

The following Christmas, I was still mourning the loss of Willie, so Freddie decided to cheer me up and gave me a little cocker spaniel named Inky Bob The Third. This gesture took quite an effort on Freddie's part, because she doesn't like dogs all that much.

Inky had a bad habit of stopping traffic by laying out in the middle of Sabathany Road, which runs by our house. When people stopped their cars, she was liable to jump up on the hood. If they opened the car, she'd been inside in a flash.

Inky was with us for about eight months before disappearing toward the end of 1989. She may have jumped in someone's car and the driver just took off.

Then we got a little grey schnauzer named Mutley from our neighbor Becky Porter. Mutley hung around the farm for four years or so, before disappearing in August 1994. After that, Freddie put her foot down and said no more dogs. Like I said, she's never really been that fond of them and never wants them in our house. Occasionally, though, Freddie will let me bring one in and hold it in my lap, but there's no walking around on the carpet or anything.

I meant to keep my promise to her, but in September 1994, I went over to this lady's house to deliver some firewood, and she showed me this little female dog. The lady said someone had abandoned the dog on her porch and she didn't know who or why. She said she couldn't keep the dog, and I said, "Well, there's no way we can let it go out on its own. It will never survive."

The little black dog wasn't friendly and wouldn't let me get near her when I delivered the first half-cord. But when I went back with the second half-cord, I took some Cheetos and lured her over. She jumped into my arms. "Tell you what," I told the lady, "how about if I take this pooch and give her a good home?"

I named the dog Oleo. When I brought her back to the farm, Freddie gave me the dickens. She was ticked off at me, Oleo, and, most of all, at the lady who started the whole thing.

I told Freddie that I need to have a dog on the farm. The reason is, if I am out there cutting wood and a tree falls and kills me, I need something to say goodbye to.

Freddie finally gave in and let me keep Oleo, who is a really good little girl, despite her bad habit of running in front of my pickup truck. Unfortunately, the life expectancy of my farm dogs hasn't been very good.

All in all, our lives together on the farm for the past eight-plus years have been pretty quiet and low-key. We just tend to our own affairs and let things go at that. Some people might say our lives are uneventful, or dull, at least compared with other folks'. They wouldn't be off the mark, either.

But that's the way Freddie and I like things to be. We don't have to be going places or spending money to be occupied. We'd rather be at home with each other than doing anything else. I'm sure we can't be the only couple in the world that feels this same way.

Freddie and I love our families, but we don't make a practice of seeing them too often, although Freddie does talk to her daughters nearly every day. It's just that we're both loners and prefer being alone together (if that makes sense). We depend a lot on each other and understand the way the other feels. We just handle things a lot better, if we're together.

Both Freddie and I were raised in good Christian homes. Though I haven't attended church in years, having spent more than enough time sitting in church pews all those years growing up, I believe in God and trust in the Bible. Freddie does too.

Freddie says God has forgiven us for our divorces, just as he forgives any of our sins each day of our lives, if we ask. Freddie also says that my making the Senior PGA Tour is God's way of showing other people that through hard work and dedication, and with God's helping hand, miracles can happen.

Nearly everywhere we've gone on the Senior PGA Tour so far in 1995, people have asked us about our cattle. We tell them that Freddie's daughters Vicky and Lisa, and Lisa's husband, H.L. Rose, are tending to them. Freddie's grandchildren—Melissa, Tiffany,

> *
> **...MAKING THE SENIOR PGA TOUR IS GOD'S WAY OF SHOWING OTHER PEOPLE THAT THROUGH HARD WORK AND DEDI- CATION, AND WITH GOD'S HELPING HAND, MIRACLES CAN HAPPEN.**

Trina and Jennifer—and my old pal, Lonnie Corley, are also available to help.

Freddie and I finally came up with a plan that may smooth things out for everyone. Before we headed out for the long swing of events between April and October, we put different colors of spray paint on each of our 15 baby calves. We used red for May, green for June, blue for July and so on, and that way the kids will know which calves need to be sold and by what date.

We're just hoping the spray paint won't wear off, and the kids won't having any problem knowing what to do with each calf. Otherwise, it can be a bit confusing, because a lot of baby calves look fairly similar to people who don't know them.

We do have the cows branded in case any of them gets out of the pasture or escapes, like Winnie did. Our brand is an "F" for Freddie and a backward "R" for Robert. I put the "R" backward because that's the way I do things on the farm.

Like I said, the cows are part of our little family. I'm sure we'll miss them and worry about them while we're gone. After all, they depend on Freddie and me to feed them and water them and, if need be, doctor them. No one knows them like we do. We can tell if one is sick or missing.

Spending all the time on the farm has helped me a great deal, not only physically but also mentally. I'm much happier, and at peace with things, now that I'm working outdoors. Also, having a practice area for golf in my own front yard has made it easy for me to hit hundreds of golf balls each day. The cows will keep the grass chewed down to where the lies aren't so bad. Of course, you can always tell when a golf ball lands in one of the cow patties: It won't bounce.

Like I said earlier, until I headed out for the 1995 Senior PGA Tour, we had been as contented as our cows. If it turns out that I don't have a long run in professional golf, it's not like we won't have anywhere to turn. Freddie and I will be more than happy to come back home to our little farm, to the way we were.

Chapter Nine

HITTING THE COMEBACK TRAIL

I remember writing a note to Freddie in 1987 that said "Fred, all my life all I have ever heard was what I couldn't do. That is exactly why I am like I am. I am an insecure, self-conscious person. Thank God for a few good things that have come my way that give me determination and courage. You are the best gift, the most strengthening and soothing."

"Golf is another," I continued. "Everyone I knew would try to discourage me. Golf may be on hold right now, but I have plans for the future that include a lot of it. That is two or three years down the road. I can be patient and get the rest leveled out and settled."

By the end of 1990, the other parts of my life had, indeed, leveled out and settled. Freddie and I were married. We had built our new house. We both had steady jobs, hers at Medical Designs and mine at Mitchell's. Life on the farm had established a peaceful, easy pace.

I was also feeling pretty good physically. My back hadn't given me any trouble in years, ever since I started doing all the manual labor associated with farm chores. So by the beginning of 1991, with everything in order, I started making plans for a comeback in competitive golf. By competitive golf, I mean significant tournaments. I had been playing in some local club events in the North Texas area during the period from 1985 through 1990, but that's not the same thing.

One of my favorites on the Texas Barbecue Circuit, as small-town Texas golf tournaments are commonly called, was the annual member-guest tournament at Holiday Hills Country Club in Mineral Wells. Jerry Hamilton, who's now my business manager, invited me to be his guest shortly after he came by Mitchell's to write a story for the *Azle News*.

Jerry stepped into my office and saw some of the scorecards I kept pinned up to the wall. Scorecards with numbers like 63 at Pecan Valley and Z. Boaz, and 64 at Singin' Hills. His eyes got real wide when he saw the 29s I'd shot at Grand Prairie, playing with Keith Flatt, and at Z. Boaz, where on the back nine, the day I shot 63.

I told Jerry all about the Sertoma golf tournament I was planning for Azle. Then I asked if he wanted to follow me down to the pro shop at Z. Boaz, where I had to deliver some clubs I'd regripped. I told him we might be able to get in a little golf, which we did.

We played a quick nine holes. Jerry seemed a bit surprised when I showed up on the first tee with a dingy little golf bag, no head covers on my woods and wearing loafers with leather soles. He asked me if I wanted him to take the golf cart out to the parking lot, so I could get my golf shoes out of the truck.

"Aw, that's okay," I said. "I'll just play in these."

I shot four-under that afternoon, with birdies on three of the first four holes. Jerry later admitted he'd been somewhat skeptical about the scorecards he'd seen in my office. That skepticism increased when he saw me walking up to the Z. Boaz clubhouse, looking like a rank beginner, but his skepticism disappeared after a few holes.

Naturally, Jerry wanted to show me off to his buddies at his home course in Mineral Wells, or, perhaps I should say, that he wanted to win some bets with his buddies. He brought me over to Mineral Wells as his designated hitter.

Holiday Hills is a short course, only about 6,100 yards or so, but you have to be plenty accurate with your irons to hit those tiny little greens. The greens slope from back to front, meaning they are really receptive to my low shots. The greens over there always seem to be in excellent condition, rolling smooth and true.

We played that first year, which was 1986, in a two-man scramble and won. I played okay, nothing special, but we brother-in-lawed it real well. Over the next few years, Jerry and I never lost a single tournament, either two-man best balls or scrambles, that we entered in Mineral Wells.

* I SHOT FOUR-UNDER THAT AFTERNOON, WITH BIRDIES ON THREE OF THE FIRST FOUR HOLES.

We had this system worked out: He would pay the entry fee, $125 per team, and I would pay him back from my half of our winnings. Never once did I have to come up with any cash. Jerry always made his own bets—I don't gamble at golf—but he was nice enough to cut me in on his winnings.

As far as the barbecue part of the deal, I was usually long gone by the time all the eating and drinking and socializing began. Having never had an alcoholic beverage in my life, I'm not much for hanging out in the 19th hole or hanging around the beer keg on the patio. That's just not my style. As soon as the golf round was over, and the scores were posted, I was back on the road to our farm outside Azle—headed back to Freddie.

In 1987, the second year I played at Holiday Hills with Jerry, we shot a best-ball of 59, 12-under par. I had 61 on my own ball, my lowest 18-hole score before or since. As I recall, I played with my burned irons. On the front nine, I started with birdies on the first three holes. After a par on number four, I made a birdie at five, an eagle on six (a par-5) and a birdie on seven, which put me seven-under after seven holes. Then at eight, one of the easiest holes on the entire course (a short par-5 reachable with driver and mid-iron), I messed up and made par. Another par at nine gave me 29 on the front side. I had another scorecard to add to my sub-30 collection pinned to the wall at my office.

On the back nine, I parred 10, birdied 11 and bogied 12 (Jerry made a 15-footer for par, helping us save a stroke). I then made birdies at 13, 14 and 15—taking me to 10-under and giving me an outside shot at the 50s.

That possibility disappeared right away, after I made par at 16 and bogey at 17 (where Jerry made another clutch par putt). I finished with a birdie at 18, however, to get back to 10-under. We beat the field by seven shots, the second-best score that day being 66. After that round, Jerry said I started running players out of the championship flight. Some of them right out of the tournament.

Jerry and I also played in some Texas Barbecue Circuit events in Jacksboro (we didn't win either time we entered, but finished in the money both times), at Runaway Bay near Bridgeport and at Live Oak in Weatherford. We won at Runaway Bay and Live Oak.

I was also playing occasionally during this period with Roland Sparks, my old friend and, as of 1995, my new caddy. We played together in some tournaments at Decatur, Nocona, Springtown and Ennis. We also played one year in the Halloween Tournament at Jacksboro. Roland and I usually finished in the top three or four, but I don't remember ever winning much.

One time, though, Roland and I did win a four-man scramble tournament at Nocona Municipal. Our partners that day were John Stuard, a policeman from Saginaw, and Lee Stinson, who's in the construction business in Fort Worth. I can also recall winning the four-man scramble at Holiday Hills. Jerry Hamilton and I were joined by Randy Couch, the golf coach at Richland High School in Fort Worth, and Jerry Ray, a lawyer in Mineral Wells, who's also the District Attorney in Palo Pinto County.

We shot 19-under the first day and 18-under the second day. We hammered everybody. But again, the course really suited my game. It seems I'd shoot at least 66 or 67 on my own ball every time out, and I'd hit enough balls close to the hole to give Jerry, or any of my scramble partners, good putts for birdie.

The course in Mineral Wells certainly isn't the toughest around, but that's not all bad. I think more golfers should play a variety of

courses, easy as well as hard. I think any golfer should find a few easier golf courses where they can post a low number, compared to their
average score. For one thing, a low score will do wonders for your
confidence. For another, when you get in a situation back at your
home course, say the annual club championship, you'll be better able
to sustain a good round. You'll have the experience under your belt
of being somewhere around par, or maybe even under par, and you'll
know what that kind of pressure feels like.

Later, Jerry Hamilton started pairing me with some of his pals.
I won the Holiday Hills best-ball twice with Jerry Ray, who's prob-
ably a 10-handicap or so, and once with Rodney Henderson, a
Mineral Wells banker, who's maybe a 12-handicap.

Holiday Hills has always been a favorite place of mine. Besides
having a fun golf course, there are some good players over there,
guys like Bill McGaha, Skipper Strickland, Pete Jones and, of
course, Jerry Hamilton. And there's a lady named Clara Robinson,
who serves up some of the best food you've ever put in your mouth.

Pete Jones, who's a farrier, meaning he shoes horses for a living, is a real hoot. He has his own way with words. Pete once saw
a guy on the practice range at Holiday Hills who was hitting shots
both left-handed and right-handed. Pete went into the clubhouse
and told the guys to come out and watch the only "amphibious"
golfer he had ever seen.

Another time, Jerry Hamilton and Pete were trying to get all
the bets straight on the first tee, when someone shouted to Pete
they weren't going to play the game he was proposing.

Pete responded, "I can't believe you guys are questioning my
integra." Skipper Strickland piped up and said, "When did you
start driving a car, Pete? I thought you still had your pickup truck."

I'll tell you one other thing about Pete Jones. He's a great putter. He's been the club champion at Holiday Hills, and I remember
winning the four-man scramble with him on two different occa-
sions. Once, we were playing with Jerry Hamilton and Rusty
Young, and we shot something like 20-under. The other time we
were playing with Jerry and his twin brother, Terry Hamilton.

The reason Pete's in the money so much is mainly because he makes everything that he looks at on those greens. The same thing happened to me in Mineral Wells when I played there in the Ram Classic in October 1994. I was paired in the four-man scramble with Ray Hott, Dale Hott and Satch Dunlap, three good guys but pretty high-handicap players. Anyway, we shot 60, 11-under, and my putter was hotter than a jalapeno pepper. I also learned something new that day: It's possible to drink beer and putt at the same time. Satch Dunlap demonstrated that technique.

Anyway, in 1991, I made my comeback in competitive golf. I turned 47 that year, and along about July I got to thinking seriously about playing in some events. Down the road, I could see myself entering tournaments like the U.S. Senior Amateur or U.S. Senior Open, so I figured I had three years to sharpen my game. As I mentioned before, professional golf really wasn't on the horizon.

That July, Steve Sosebee sold me back the irons I'd built for him. That sparked my interest in practicing, and I spent a couple of months getting reacquainted with those clubs. One day that summer Gary Clark, who's with Clark Precision Machine and Tool in Azle, came into Mitchell's. I asked him to make me a putter, and he said he'd make one for each of us. I drew up a design on a piece of paper, and he took it back to the shop. When the guys in the machine shop were making the club, though, they got the putterhead on backwards. Rather than start the job over, they just heated up the neck of club and twisted it so the face would be right. So now I had a customized "twist" putter to go along with burned irons.

Gary tried to apologize for the way the club looked, but I wouldn't hear any of it. I liked the way that putter looked. "Hey, that's the best thing you could have done," I told him. "Now I have a really special club." I putted really well all year with my special twist putter. Come to think of it, maybe I should bring it out of the closet.

That Labor Day, I entered the Fort Worth City Championship for the first time in years. In the first round, I shot 70 at the Hills Course at Pecan Valley, which put me in the top five, after which I did a little interview with Charles Clines of the *Fort Worth Star-Telegram*. In the second round, I shot 74 on the River Course at Pecan Valley, which dropped me back to even par. I'd lost contact with the leaders. The final round was at Meadowbrook, and I shot 76 and finished 12th. Overall, I wasn't very happy with my performance, and probably would have pulled out of the Texas State Open qualifying if I hadn't already sent in the entry fee.

Later that September, I drove over to Lost Creek, which had changed a good bit from its days as Singin' Hills, and shot 72. I finished fourth, which was good enough to qualify. The round at Lost Creek made me feel pretty good, coming as it did right after my disappointing showing in the Fort Worth tournament.

Before the 1991 Texas State Open at Firewheel Golf Park in Garland, on the northeast side of Dallas, I got my uncle, Tommy McDaniel, to drive me over for a practice round. I found out there are 36 holes at Firewheel, so later I drove back over and played a second practice round. I discovered that I liked the Old Course at Firewheel more than the Lakes Course, probably because it's a flatter course and better fits my game.

My goal at the 1991 Texas State Open was just to make it through four rounds. I learned we had a 90-player cut, which is very generous, instead of the usual 60-player cut, which obviously puts more pressure on you at the start. I opened with a 72, one-over, on the Lakes Course, making three birdies right quick to steady myself. The significant thing about that day was on the seventh hole, I hit a tee shot with my Wilson Staff TC2 ball that hit a cart path. That scuffed up my ball, so I took it out of play on the next tee and changed to another Wilson. Then from the eighth hole of the first round through the first hole of the fourth round, I played with the same ball. That's more than two-and-a-half rounds (47 holes) with one ball.

The reason I didn't change balls was because I was playing pretty good with that one. In the second round, I shot 74, two-over at the Old Course. My three-over total allowed me to make the cut with room to spare, and I noticed they had five gift certificates and three trophies for the amateurs. I checked the board and saw that only seven amateurs had made the cut, so I knew right then I'd probably see some sort of return. I was second low amateur, trailing only Richard Ellis, who plays out of Plano.

In the third round, I shot 71, one-under, on the Old Course course, and moved ahead of Ellis, who slipped to 75. The last day on the par-5 on the 13th hole, I hit a driver and 4-wood to the green and rolled in a 35-foot putt for eagle. That set me up to get to the clubhouse. I made one bogey (a three-putt) and one birdie coming in.

My closing 71 gave me 288 for the tournament, one-over par. That was four shots better than Larry Thomas, who's from Dallas, and seven ahead of Ellis. I finished in 39th place overall, well behind the winner, Mike Peck. When I was presented the trophy for being low amateur, I put that golf ball that I'd used for 47 holes into the cup. I remember having to go to a junk auction in La Junta that night. I got there late, but it was fun to walk in and tell Freddie, Vicky and Lisa what I had done.

ON THE PAR-5 13TH HOLE, I HIT A DRIVER AND 4-WOOD TO THE GREEN AND ROLLED IN A 35-FOOT PUTT FOR EAGLE.

That performance in the Texas State Open pretty well set me up to play golf again. I knew I was on the comeback trail. I felt I had been fortunate to win the low amateur honors in that tournament. All the years, all the trials and all the hard work trying to achieve something in golf had taught me how very difficult something like that really is. To come back and accomplish something like that in my first Texas State Open in years, and only my second tournament in 1991, told me I was extremely blessed.

Being low amateur certainly wasn't something I expected, and really and truly, more than feeling like the beginning of something, it felt like at least it would be a nice end to something. From that standpoint, I was encouraged a lot, but not overly optimistic.

My finish in the 1991 Texas State Open earned me an exemption to the 1992 Texas State Open (at Firewheel Golf Park again, where I played poorly and missed the cut). It also earned me an invitation to play in the 1992 Texas Cup matches, which the *Dallas Morning News* had decided to start up again after a long suspension.

The Texas Cup Matches, which pit 12 Texas pros against 12 Texas amateurs, were a pretty big deal back in the 1930s, 1940s and 1950s. Some of the really great players from Texas, Byron Nelson among them, played in the Texas Cup years ago.

The *Dallas Morning News* Texas Cup Matches took place on November 2-3, 1992 at the Four Seasons Resort and Club in Irving. The TPC-Las Colinas course is the site of one of the most popular tournaments on the PGA Tour, the GTE Byron Nelson Classic.

I had the chance to be a teammate of some of the best amateurs in the state. Guys like Chip Stewart and Bink Mitchella from Dallas, Bill Holstead of Wichita Falls, Richard Ellis from Plano, David Ojala and Randy Sonnier from Houston, Rich Mayo from El Paso, Mike Hoyle from Austin and John Grace from Fort Worth. Our nonplaying captain was Bill Penn, director of the Texas Golf Association.

We were going up against some of the top club pros in the state, including J.L. Lewis from Round Rock, Terry Dear from Lubbock, Robert Hoyt from Dallas, Lindy Miller from Fort Worth, Benny Passons from Kemp, and Dudley Wysong from McKinney. Their nonplaying captain was Ross Collins, the long time pro at Dallas Athletic Club.

We gave the pros a good run for the money, losing the Ryder Cup-style format (24 points) by a score of 13-11. We even had the lead after the first day of play, 6 1/2 to 5 1/2. Maybe the Texas amateurs could have pulled a big upset on the Texas pros, if only the farmer from Azle had done a little bit better. In my three matches, two partnership events and one singles, I got shut out. No excuses, I just never got in a good rhythm. I spent the whole time trying to recover from mistakes.

In the four-ball event the first morning, Mike Hoyle and I lost to Gary Dennis of Fort Worth and David Lundstrom of Houston, 4 and 3. In the foursome (alternate shot) match that afternoon, Mike and I teamed up again, and this time we were defeated by Lindy

Miller and Robert Hoyt, 3 and 2.

I've always liked watching Robert, who was part of that U.S. Open qualifier sudden-death playoff at Shady Valley in 1980, just because of how far he hits the ball. He's awesome. I didn't especially enjoy seeing him play that day, though.

In the singles match the next day, I lost 4 and 3 to Ken McDonald of Bay Oaks in Houston. My game was never a factor. I just never got in the sync of playing.

By the time the 1992 Texas Cup Matches rolled around, I had lost my job with Mitchell's Department Stores. I'd been with the company for 20 years—longer than that, really, if you count the time I worked at the Lake Worth store during high school and at the East Belknap store in Fort Worth during my days at TCU.

After several years of declining sales volume at the Azle store, Mitchell's management finally decided to shut it down. Within a few months, by the beginning of 1993, all the stores had closed.

By then, shopping patterns had changed, once and for all. People liked the convenience of doing one-stop shopping at malls. Kids liked hanging out in the malls. Senior citizens could walk around in the air-conditioned malls. Everybody could eat meals at the mall. You could spend practically all day at the mall, hitting all the various stores, rather than have to drive around from place to place to do your shopping. That put a lot of pressure on stand-alone stores like Mitchell's.

So did the emergence of the superstores, like K-Mart and WalMart, where you can find practically everything under the sun, from hardwares and appliances to records and tapes to clothes and home furnishings.

At Mitchell's, we only sold one thing: clothes. Though we had real loyal customers in Azle, we just didn't have enough of them to keep us going. By the time the store closed, I only had eight employees, and they were all hourly workers. A large part of my job was juggling their work schedules. We didn't need all of them, all of the time, to handle our traffic flow. Which, towards the end, was more like a traffic trickle.

I was sad to see the store close, of course. It had served the community well for many, many years. I was sad for my Uncle Wilburn, who had invested his life in the company. At least he had a good, long ride. And I was sad for the long-time employees, people like Geneva Pruitt, Geneva Stevens, Del Hamilton, Raye White and Mack Pickard, the shoe clerk, and especially someone like Daisy Bailey, who depended on her job to make enough of a living to raise her kids.

I wasn't all that sad for myself, however. In truth, I probably needed some kind of change. I was pretty well burned-out on my job at Mitchell's, having put in all the 60-hour weeks I cared to. I was tired of the corporate structure and ready for the freedom of being on my own.

I was the last one out at Mitchell's in September 1992 and turned off the lights. Actually, I stayed around for a couple of weeks after the official store closing, just cleaning up the place and getting rid of things. I made a deal with Mitchell's to haul off some scrap wood and shelving, which I put to use at the farm.

From the Texas Cup Matches in November 1992, until I turned fifty, fourteen months later, my golf was pretty uneventful. I tried to qualify for the 1993 Texas State Open in August, but missed out at Fossil Creek in Fort Worth. I had a chance until I double-bogeyed the 18th hole. After hitting my second shot on the par-5 into a sand trap about 90 yards from the green, I shanked one out of there into the trees by the cart path. From there I punched a shot over the green into a bunker, blasted out onto the green and two-putted for seven.

That was very much out of character for me. I have a pretty good track record in qualifying events. Generally in those situations, I can keep my score around par, and that's usually enough. I concentrate on keeping the ball in play, in the fairways and on the greens, and when I do miss a green, I usually still have a chance to save par. Playing golf like that, you make only a few bogeys. You seldom shoot a really big number, either, like double-bogey or worse, which is typically what ruins the chances of the guys who don't qualify. They have one or two really big numbers—and then they're gone.

Maybe the reason my golf game was nothing special between the time Mitchell's closed and 1994 was that in those days I was busy trying to figure out a way to make a living.

One thing I tried my hand at was second-hand sales. I was your basic junk man, sort of like a Fred Sanford without the store. I'd fill up my pickup truck with stuff I'd bought at garage sales in and around Azle. Then I'd try to resell the stuff at flea markets out on the Jacksboro Highway, or over in Weatherford, at First Monday. First Monday is a huge flea market that occurs on the first weekend of the month. The one in Weatherford is pretty well known, and there's one in Canton, east of Dallas, that's an even bigger deal. Why it's referred to as First Monday is beyond me, because it all happens on Friday, Saturday and Sunday.

Here's how I'd accumulate stuff to sell: I'd buy a copy of the *Azle News* on Wednesday night and see where all the garage sales would be on Thursday, Friday and Saturday. I'd map out a route that would allow me to cover as much ground as possible in the shortest amount of time. It's funny, but you'd always see the same 20 or 30 people at garage sales. You had to get there early, and figure out what the good buys were, or these people, the "pros" as Freddie and I liked to call them, would beat you to it. The hard part was that there just weren't that many good buys at any one sale.

I quickly learned that the trick in the flea market business is not to buy too much stuff. You shouldn't tie up too much money in things you might not be able to unload. Not that I had much money to tie up in the first place. I used to come across some pretty good deals on riding lawn mowers, which were selling in the $400-$500 range. If I could have bought them, I'm pretty sure I could have resold them for a $100 or $150 profit. But I never had the $400 or so to put in them in the first place.

I had my best luck buying little glass animals and glass or wood birds. There was always a market for them. I also bought a lot of brass items and old Avon bottles. I still have 300 or 400 of those bottles lying around, so I suppose I miscalculated the demand for them.

I also liked to buy old tennis shoes for 50 cents and old jeans for $1 a pair. As a rule, I tried to keep all my purchases to $1 or less. Then I'd try to resell the same stuff for $1.50 or $2. It's a pretty hard way of doing things.

For awhile there, though, we tried to make a regular business out of it. In the spring of 1993, I became partners with a friend named John Griffin. We rented space in the Ash Creek Plaza on the Jacksboro Highway. My dad gave me $1,300 to put into the business, and we spent that amount renting space and fixing the place up. I took my golf club repair stuff down there, as well, hoping to pick up a little business.

We never had any real luck selling stuff. When the summer of 1993 rolled around, John, who's a retired guy with a mobile home, decided to take off for the open road. I could have kept the business open, but after looking at the books, I decided to shut down. We weren't setting the world on fire.

I still kept a hand in the flea market business for awhile, though, renting space in Weatherford for First Monday. I'd rent two booths for $60 and try to sell all the stuff I'd accumulated here or there. I sold some of the cow knickknacks Freddie and I had made out of bowling pins. I also tried selling golf clubs that I'd repaired and restored, but I never had much luck with that. I guess not too many golfers hang out at flea markets.

> *
>
> **ONE THING I TRIED**
>
> **MY HAND AT WAS**
>
> **SECOND-HAND**
>
> **SALES. I WAS**
>
> **YOUR BASIC JUNK**
>
> **MAN, SORT OF**
>
> **LIKE A FRED**
>
> **SANFORD WITHOUT**
>
> **THE STORE.**

Also in the summer of 1993, I started cutting firewood to sell the following fall and winter. I did a lot of the cutting up around Poolville, where a pipeline had been pushed away. I stacked up a pretty good inventory of seasoned wood, much of which I was able to sell the following winter.

I probably handled about 15 or 20 chain saws in 1993 and 1994. Most were ones I'd bought at garage sales that had seen their best day. I was trying to squeeze a little more life out of them, but that strategy didn't work too well, so I moved up in class to a 20" Poulan and flat wore out that chain saw.

I finally bit the bullet and paid $400 for a new 16" Stihl chain saw. I bought that one because that's the brand professionals use, according to a buddy who's a Stihl dealer. You know how that works.

Between flea market sales, cutting wood and a little golf repair business, I managed to eke out a living. Freddie, though, lost her job at Medical Designs late in 1993, after tendinitis in her wrist and elbow got so bad that she couldn't work on the assembly line any longer. She had been making something like $132 a week, and we missed the income.

That's about where we were when I turned 50 in January 1994 and we started the steps leading up to the Senior PGA Tour.

Looking back, one of the most important rounds of golf I played during 1994 was the Texas State Open qualifier in August. I returned to Fossil Creek, where I flubbed things up the year before. On the par-3 on the 4th hole, a really tough hole, I rolled in a 60-foot putt for birdie. That gave me the spark that set up my entire round. I shot 72, earning a ticket to Houston.

On the 18th hole, where I made double-bogey in 1993, I got revenge. I hit a good drive, a solid 1-iron and, making up for the shanked third shot the year before, I hit a 70-yard sand wedge to within six inches of the hole. Believe me, that was a really sweet tap-in birdie.

When I went to the 1994 Texas State Open at The Woodlands near Houston, I still wasn't 100 percent sure what my plans would be. But making the cut there gave me a big boost in confidence, a real shot in the arm. It was exactly the kind of encouragement I needed to go ahead and attempt the Senior PGA Tour qualifying, which took me to San Antonio and, ultimately, Tampa.

And the rest, as they say, is history.

Chapter Ten

HOMETOWN HERO

Ever since I qualified for the 1995 Senior PGA Tour last fall, people in and around Azle have been extremely supportive and encouraging to Freddie and me. Not that I'm suggesting they weren't real nice before. They were.

But in the last six months people have come up and told us how happy they are for us, especially those folks familiar with how much we were struggling before this windfall happened, and those who know how much time and energy I've devoted to the game of golf.

Maybe some of the Azle residents who used to wonder why I would spend my lunch hours hitting golf balls in the park realize now that it wasn't a waste of time. They would probably agree with me that all those hours were well spent.

In addition to the benefit tournament Steve Champion, Jim Laird and Steve Henton organized for us at Squaw Creek, the city fathers of Azle extended special recognition. The mayor, C.Y. (call me Cy) Rone, invited Freddie and me to ride with him in the Christmas parade in Azle last December. We drove around town in a little, red convertible Mazda Miata, that Jimmy Lynn, of Jimmy Lynn Motor Co., provided.

Several Azle residents had pooled their money and paid for a banner that stretched across Main Street. The banner—which read *"Congratulations Robert Landers, Senior PGA Tour"*—stayed up several months until a windstorm chewed it up.

On February 9, 1995, after my closely watched debut on the Senior PGA Tour, Bob Buckel, the editor and publisher of the *Azle News*, wrote one of his "Buckshots" columns about all the hoopla and media frenzy down in Florida. He said the media had jumped on me "like ducks on a Wheat Thin."

"Robert has gotten more attention over the past two weeks than President Clinton," noted Buckel, "although Clinton said more words in his State of the Union speech than Robert has said in his whole life." Buckel also called me the "anti-O.J." and described me as the opposite of most superstar heroes of sport these days.

"Robert doesn't own a Rolls Royce," he wrote. "He doesn't have a guy named Kato who lives in the guest house and looks after his pool. He's never done a commercial or been on Letterman. He's never gone on strike because he only makes $4 million a year and wants $5 million. He's never cussed his coach or tossed firecrackers at fans or charged little kids $50 for his autograph."

Buckel expressed the hope that the media crush would die down and that I could go back to playing golf in relative peace and quiet. "But doesn't it say something about the state of American sports when someone gets so famous simply for being so ordinary?" he wrote. "Robert is inspirational because he's normal."

"Yes," he concluded, "we can identify with Robert Landers. He's just like us, down to the sneakers and the sheepish grin. The only difference is that when you get him on a golf course, he can cash the checks our minds can only write."

I came home from the tour after three weeks, while some of the leading Senior PGA Tour players went to Mexico for the Chrysler Cup. On February 22, Azle celebrated the grand opening of Cross Timbers with a ribbon-cutting ceremony and golf tournament.

Among those in attendance were people involved with the development of Cross Timbers, including Jeff Brauer and

John Colligan of GolfScapes, the course architects; Dick Watson and Monte Von Seggern of Watson Golf Course Construction, the course builders; Emil Wood of Wudco Properties, who built the clubhouse and other buildings on the course.

Tim Burke of Municipal Golf Inc. of Omaha, Nebraska, the company that put together the financing arrangement, and Mike Lohner of Evergreen Alliance Golf Limited of Dallas, which manages the facility and which invested some of its money to upgrade the clubhouse facilities, were there as well.

I was asked to say a few things at the Cross Timbers grand opening. I told everyone that this was one of the proudest days of my life, which it truly was. I talked about having always had the dream to help bring golf to Azle, a dream I shared with Azle residents like Bill Brown, Kenneth Holmes, Bill Woodard and Iona Reed, big golf supporters who had since passed away, and community leaders like B.J. Clark, Ronnie Feemster and Harry Dulin, who helped make this dream become a reality.

*

"ROBERT HAS GOT-TEN MORE ATTEN-TION OVER THE PAST TWO WEEKS THAN PRESIDENT CLINTON."

I also explained that one of the reasons behind my attempting to qualify for the professional tour was that I wanted to help get Cross Timbers off to a solid start. I guessed that as a result of my success and all the national publicity my qualifying had generated, perhaps as many as five million people across America had now heard of Azle, Texas, and, in addition, about Cross Timbers. I've been trying to spread the word about Cross Timbers everywhere I go, by wearing golf shirts and sweaters with the course's name and logo.

I had tears in my eyes and a lump in my throat by the time I finished talking. That's how much seeing Cross Timbers finally completed and open for business has meant to me.

Cross Timbers is going to be an excellent golf course. It was still a little raw in places this past spring, but people who've been playing there have had nothing but nice things to say. And Carl Fisher, the head golf professional, told me recently that Cross Timbers has been getting a pretty fair amount of play. I went out

there before Easter, on Good Friday, and the parking lot was nearly full. That's real encouraging.

Cross Timbers will be closed during the summer of 1995,
while they grow in the Bermuda grass, and while they do some
pruning, sprucing and clearing out of underbrush. But the course
sits on a pretty piece of property that used to belong to the
Scrimptures, an old, established Azle family. Cross Timbers covers
some 212 acres, with plenty of gentle hills and rolling grassland and
a lot of different kinds of mature trees. It has the feeling of a Texas
Hill Country course, and once everything grows in and greens up,
it will be a beauty.

There are some tough holes at Cross Timbers, especially on
the front nine. The third is a 468-yard par-4, which plays into the
prevailing wind and which will give players everything they want.
It's kind of tight hole with a depression in front of the green, meaning the approach shot is pretty much all carry. You can't run the ball
on. For some players, it will be a three-shot hole. Par will always be
a good score there. The fourth hole, a 229-yard par-3, takes a pretty good poke to reach the green in regulation.

The signature hole at Cross Timbers is the par-3 seventh,
which plays downwind to an elevated green guarded by a handful
of pot bunkers on the front. It's rimmed at the back by a rock wall.
It's a one of those picture postcard holes.

The back nine at Cross Timbers might be a bit easier than the
front, mainly because it's about 250 yards shorter. There are some
nice holes, especially down the stretch at 16, 17 and 18. Par is 72,
36 a side. I hope anyone who's ever in the Dallas/Fort Worth area,
for business or pleasure, gets a chance to swing by Cross Timbers.
If you do, tell them Robert sent you.

Members from the media were out in full force for the grand
opening at Cross Timbers. TV news crews came from Channel 5
(NBC) in Fort Worth and Channel 4 (CBS) and Channel 8 (ABC)
in Dallas. Writers like Jimmy Burch and Charles Clines of the *Fort
Worth Star-Telegram,* Jeff Rude of the *Dallas Morning News,* and
Mike Towle with *Golf World* showed up. I also did interviews with

Glenn Mitchell with National Public Radio and Brad Bailey, a writer with *D, The Magazine of Dallas*.

I could have talked to those guys all afternoon and night about Cross Timbers. As you can probably tell, it's one of my favorite subjects. I think part of its appeal to golfers is that it's detached from the hustle and bustle of city life. It's separated from all the noise by the timber that stands around the edges of the property.

"This golf course really was Robert's dream," Freddie told one writer that day. "Playing on the professional tour came out of the blue. Cross Timbers is something he's been hoping for and working towards for years and years."

That's true. Back in 1988 or 1989, I had been asked by the Azle Parks and Recreation Board to serve on a fact-finding citizens' committee to look into getting a golf course built. David Delfeld, Robert Pauley, David Gilley, Bill Woodard, Doug Conner, Linda Scott, Ronnie Feemster, Jerry Futrell and I made up the original committee. Claude Conwell, Joann Brown and Iona Reed later joined the group, after someone dropped out.

One of the first things we did was get advice from C.A. Sanford from North Richland Hills, Texas, who was instrumental in getting that city's golf course, called Iron Horse, built. C.A. informed us about all the paperwork required and gave us tips on things to avoid in the process. He helped out a great deal.

After several starts and stops over the next few years, including a couple of feasibility studies and a time-out while the city had a referendum on the golf course project, which carried pretty easily, we got the job done. While we were involved with the project, the city coincidentally found out it had to upgrade the standards of its wastewater management. Pumping wastewater onto a new golf course for irrigation purposes gave Azle a money-saving alternative to the expense of upgrading its water treatment facilities to meet the tougher standards. Spending $3.5 million to build a public golf course was a real bargain compared with spending $5 million to comply with the new codes.

Tom Brace, a geologist who sat in on some of our meetings as a volunteer, was the guy who hit on the name of Cross Timbers. He pointed out that's what this part of North Texas is called. The Cross Timbers region serves as the buffer zone between wet East Texas and arid West Texas. The Cross Timbers logo, a chapparal (or road-runner), was designed by Paul Quinones of Todd Company in Arlington, Texas.

One of the most gratifying parts of the grand opening at Cross Timbers was seeing several kids I used to know who now have jobs in the cart barn or pro shop. These are kids who had participated years ago in some of my summer golf clinics. Beginning around 1980, I started organizing week-long golf clinics for kids through Sertoma Club. I wanted Azle youngsters to get exposed to the game of golf, an opportunity I didn't have as a boy.

I think golf is one of the best sports for kids of all ages, simply because it teaches them honor and discipline. It teaches kids how to deal with adversity and helps them develop self-reliance. Golf is always trying your patience—and if there's one thing kids today probably need to learn it's patience. So many of them, it seems, always want things their own way—and they want things now. Golf, or life, simply doesn't work that way. You have to earn your rewards, they aren't just handed over to you. And there's no shortcut to success.

I remember that for one of the early clinics, I talked the Azle public schools into letting me use some school buses. We transported kids down to Rockwood Park in Fort Worth, and the pro down there, Dick Weston, helped me get enough clubs for everyone. Dick rounded up pros from other city courses, and some of his assistants, to help conduct the clinics. Other years, we've also had clinics at the Casino Beach Golf Academy in Lake Worth.

I probably wouldn't have taken the initiative to stage the clinics, or junior golf tournaments, without my experiences in Sertoma, which brought me out of my shell and taught me how to give back to my community. And I might not have done them without the example set years ago by Jim Bob Nation.

Back when I was growing up, the one guy who always took the lead in getting youth baseball leagues organized in Azle was Jim

Bob Nation, a local insurance agent. He was the guy who had the time and energy, and the devotion to kids and sports, to make things happen.

Jim Bob had played some professional ball when he was younger, but he was injured falling out of a pecan tree and had to hang up his spikes. Being an aspiring baseball player myself, I thought Jim Bob Nation hung the moon. As far as Azle goes, he was probably as close to a legendary person as I thought there ever was, or ever would be. I remember that Sertoma named him Azle's "Citizen of the Year," and I couldn't have been happier for him.

If I could touch the lives of a few kids the way Jim Bob touched ours, I'd be awfully proud. One of my goals in golf has been to introduce the game to as many people, especially youngsters, as I can.

A couple days after the Cross Timbers grand opening, where I used an axe to cut the ribbon on the bridge leading across Ash Creek to the golf course and hit the ceremonial first ball, Azle State Bank invited me and Freddie down for a little gathering. Carl Campbell, the bank president, and Tim Carpenter, the loan officer, had put together a promotion called "Banking on the Green" to show their support for Cross Timbers and, I suppose, me.

They had the bank lobby and walls decorated with pictures of me and with golfing stuff. I signed autographs and Freddie and I mingled with a lot of old friends. The bank promotion drew a good crowd and seemed to go over pretty well.

In early April, when I came home from the tour for several weeks, North Texas still had out the welcome mat. I received an invitation to participate in a charity golf tournament hosted by Scott Murray, the sports anchor on Channel 5 in Fort Worth, and Bob Lilly, the former NFL All-Pro lineman. Bob Lilly was always one of my favorite players when he was with the Dallas Cowboys, and I asked him for his autograph.

I was also invited by Supreme Golf, the Fort Worth golf retail-chain, to make an appearance at its new superstore in Southlake, Texas, just west of the Dallas/Fort Worth Airport. I spent one evening there shaking hands and meeting golf fans. That's one of the nicest golf retail stores I've ever seen. It has a super large indoor putting green, and that's something I could use: a little practice with the putter.

I was also asked by the Texas Tire Dealers Association to appear at their annual convention, which was in Fort Worth. As part of the convention, the group had a golf outing at Iron Horse Golf Club and I played a couple holes with each group.

I hit drives and approach shots for them on the par-5 11th hole at Iron Horse, which gave me a chance to practice with a new Cubic Balance 48" driver I'd been trying. I was hitting the ball pretty well that day, averaging 265 yards, but a tire dealer named Jeff Young showed me up by busting a drive 285 yards. That must have got my goat, because I immediately cranked one 290 yards.

A HIGHER TRAJECTORY IS ONE THING I NEED ON THE SENIOR PGA TOUR.

Also while I was home, I met with Barney Adams of Adams Golf in Dallas, who had offered to build a set of clubs to my specifications. Barney guaranteed his clubs would enable me to get more height on my shots, which is crucial. A higher trajectory is one thing I need on the Senior PGA Tour, because many of the courses we play have elevated greens. The only way to get your ball to check is with a high, soft shot. Which, as you know by now, has never been my strength.

I met with Barney and his chief clubfitter, Max Puglielli, once over in Dallas and once at Leonard Golf Links in Fort Worth, a great practice facility with a western theme. They got the shafts of the Assault irons set to the right stiffness, and I started hitting them really solid.

I also got in a few practice rounds. I played twice at Hackberry Creek in Irving, once with Jerry Hamilton and once in a foursome with Dick Goetz, a Senior PGA Tour player from Dallas, Bill Garrett, the Ping rep in this area, and Mike Peck, the Spalding rep. Local qualifying for the 1995 Senior U.S. Open will be at Hackberry Creek in mid-June, and I wanted a sneak preview so I could come up with a game plan.

I also played the Cottonwood Valley course at the Four Seasons Resort and Club in Irving. I played the Ridglea and Mira Vista country clubs in Fort Worth. Everywhere I went, people gathered around to watch, which made me feel really good. Jerry started calling me the "Pied Piper" of the golf course.

I also got in tuneup rounds for the Dallas Reunion Pro-Am, which is scheduled for the second weekend in June. I've asked Phil Lumsden, a golf buddy as far back as the early 1970s, when we were competing against each other in the Fort Worth City Championship, to join me. Phil and I played Oak Cliff Country Club, a tree-lined, traditional kind of course, with two Dallas club pros, Ronny Glanton and Billy Harris. They were good guys and good players.

I also played once with Russell Orth, the head pro at Oak Cliff. He and John Denton, tournament manager of the Dallas Reunion Pro-Am have been extremely nice to me and have made me feel right at home.

One day in late April, Jerry and I drove down to Phil's course in Dennis, Texas, called Sugar Tree. That's one of my favorite golf courses in Texas, not just because Phil built it himself, but also because it's a good test. Sugar Tree is really tight off the tee, and you'd better bring your "A" game or be prepared to suffer the consequences.

I played Sugar Tree quite a few times over the past few years, paying the twilight rate of $10 and carrying my own bag. Late in the day, you can see plenty of deer foraging around the fairways, which is a soothing, tranquil sight. I enjoy deer a great deal more now that Freddie has convinced me to stop hunting them.

Another reason I like Sugar Tree so much is that because it's such a tight driving course, you can always find plenty of golf balls people have lost in the woods. Roland Sparks and I used to drive down there early on Tuesday morning, just to have first shot at all the lost golf balls from the weekend traffic. I bet we averaged finding 75 to 100 balls, which I could turn around and sell at flea markets in Azle or Weatherford.

I won't have to set up shop again at the flea markets anytime soon, however. Jerry Hamilton began negotiating a two-year contract with Lectronic Kaddy, a company based in Canada that makes a remote-controlled bag carrier. In exchange for having the Lectronic Kaddy name on my golf bag, and the side of my cap, I'll earn a small percentage of the company's annual sales in 1995 and 1996 and get a small ownership position. Also, an oilman in Houston, Frank Wade, paid us $25,000 for a shirt endorsement. I'll wear the name of his company, F.W. Oil, on the sleeve of my golf shirt.

About the only disappointment on the home front, and a minor one, really, was that I didn't receive an invitation to play in the 1995 Colonial National Invitation in Fort Worth.

Not that I deserved to have a spot in a PGA Tour event, or anything. Back in February, I had written to Floyd Wade, Colonial's tournament chairman, asking to be considered for one of the handful of sponsor's invitations. I didn't expect to receive one, but I figured it never hurts to ask.

Jerry thought we had a chance to get in the field, just because of the gate potential. So many people in and around Fort Worth have read about me, or heard about me, but so few have actually seen me play, that Jerry seemed to think I could help sell a few tickets to the tournament. Although with the quality fields they always get in Fort Worth, and with a defending champion like Nick Price, the PGA Tour's two-time Player-of-the-Year, I don't suppose the Colonial folks have had any trouble selling tickets.

I knew my chances for an invitation were slim to none, just because the Colonial probably wants those invitations to go to up-and-coming PGA Tour players. I also knew that keeping up with the flatbellies on the PGA Tour would have been a tall order for me. Heck, I've got my hands full just trying to keep up with the rounded bellies on the Senior PGA Tour.

Of which mine is one. I've gained about 25 pounds since the 1995 Senior PGA Tour began. Part of it is probably compensating for the years I lived on soup all week, just so I could have some money for golf. Part of it is my sweet tooth. When my employees at Mitchell's wanted time off, I always tried to see that they got it, as long as they saw to it that in return I got some of their cakes, pies or puddings. Those ladies were all wonderful cooks.

Another reason for my sudden weight gain is that while I was home in April, I discovered the all-you-can-eat menu at Waffle House. I've taken to ordering a double cheeseburger with a double order of hash brown potatoes—scattered, smothered and covered. That means scattered on the plate, smothered in onions and covered in cheese. They are really delicious.

Jerry says Waffle House is the only place we've gone to in the past four months where people don't recognize me. I guess not too many golfers, or *Sports Illustrated* readers, hang out at Waffle House. And I guess the waitresses don't read the sports pages.

During the 1995 Colonial National Invitation I'll be in Pittsburgh, playing in the Quicksilver Classic, where I need to be to start climbing the 1995 Senior PGA Tour money list.

Now my pro debut in the North Texas area will come at the Dallas Reunion Pro-Am at Oak Cliff Country Club in mid-June, 1995. I'm excited about that event and really hope to do well before the home folks. I'm hoping to get to see a lot of friends from Azle and Fort Worth, as well as a bunch of golfers I've played with or against on the Texas Barbecue Circuit. It's going to be a really fun week.

Which is what 1995 has been for Freddie and me, one special occasion after another. We've had enough terrific things happen to us in the last six months to last a lifetime, or fill a book.

Or, who knows, to maybe even make a movie. One other thing that happened while we were home, besides this book contract with Harvest Media, Inc. was that Jerry made a deal with Davis Entertainment, which gave those film folks the rights to develop a movie about my life. Davis Entertainment, run by John Davis, the son of billionaire Marvin Davis, has had some blockbuster hits like "Predator" and "The Firm."

Jeffrey Fried and Adam Lenkin of Fried & Co., a legal firm in Washington, D.C. that represents actress Michelle Pfeiffer and boxing champion Riddick Bowe, helped Jerry handle the negotiations with

Davis Entertainment. Freddie and I received a small signing bonus and have the chance to make six figures, if a movie ever gets made.

I'm not sure what will happen with that project, exactly, but I know it wouldn't hurt a bit if I won a Senior PGA Tour tournament, and it wouldn't hurt any if I won in dramatic fashion, like in a sudden-death playoff with Ray Floyd, Lee Trevino, Jim Colbert, Dave Stockton or Jack Nicklaus.

It's either that, or Davis Entertainment is going to need to hire a really creative screenwriter.

Chapter Eleven

TRAVELS WITH
FREDDIE

I've been taking a few notes on the 1995 Senior PGA Tour, so Freddie and I will have a record of some of our experiences. I'm sure that in years to come, we'll look back at 1995 as one of the best times in our lives. We'd like to share some of the background:

ROYAL CARIBBEAN CLASSIC
Links at Key Biscayne, Key Biscayne, Florida
Jan. 30 - Feb. 5, 1995

From a player's standpoint, the course played really hard. The wind was a big factor for two of the three days, and the greens were fast and firm. The big problem for me was all the sand traps around the greens, as well as the fact you had to hit the ball into the greens with a really high shot that would sit down softly. My low trajectory shots didn't fit that layout real well. I did play my bunker shots pretty well, however.

The main thing I learned in Miami was that I was hitting my driver (a Taylor Made Burner Bubble) too short. I'm going to have to pick up some distance to play against these guys. I averaged something like 240 yards off the tee at Key Biscayne. That left me with too many medium (3,4,5) irons for my second shots, when other players were hitting short (6,7,8) irons.

The press in Miami had a field day with the Tour rookies from Texas. They made a big deal about Freddie getting confused and taking three hours to get to a golf course that was 10 minutes from the hotel. They joked about how I paid for ham-and-cheese sandwiches at a concession stand on the course, when there was a free buffet in the players' dining area not more than 30 yards away.

The media also had a good laugh when they reported that Freddie was not familiar with a fax. Raymond Floyd's secretary told Freddie that she would fax directions to their house, for the party, and Freddie said, "Okay, but how will I get the directions?" Everyone seemed equally amused that, when the light on the telephone in our hotel room started flashing, we called down to the front desk and asked them to please fix it. No, we didn't know that the flashing meant we had phone messages. Now we do.

A group of our friends from the North Texas area went to Miami to watch my debut, including Billy Green, Clint Hankins, Jim Laird and Charlie Green from Azle and Jay Dee Jones from Arlington. Steve Champion, his wife, Lori, and their little daughter, Katie, came down and also got to visit Steve's parents in the area. Johnny Rodriguez and George Pulido from Fort Worth were also there.

Speaking of George, when we went to dinner at Don Shula's, I knocked over a glass of water and it spilled into his lap. George, who's with the Pulido's restaurant chain based in Fort Worth, acted like nothing ever happened but I soaked him pretty good. Sorry about that, George.

At the pro-am party early in the week, Freddie showed up wearing slacks and flats. She immediately noticed that she was underdressed for the occasion. Freddie later said that from now on, if an invitation to one of these parties says "casual" attire, she's going to interpret that to mean to break out her "dressy" clothes. Me, I'll just show up in my sports jacket, which Freddie bought at Penney's for $60, and hope everything's all right.

One night early in the week, we went to dinner at the Rusty Pelican. Freddie, Jerry Hamilton, Jay Dee Jones and Charles Clines were with me. I ordered lobster for the first time in my life. When they brought it out, I looked it over, picked it up by the claw and asked Jerry, "Okay, how do you eat this thing?" Lobsters are a lot of work, but they taste pretty good.

SCORES: 75-79-74/228 (15 over)

FINISH: 62 (tie)

EARNINGS: $1,275

THE INTELLINET CHALLENGE
The Vineyards, Naples, Florida
Feb. 6 - 12

The golf course in Naples, The Vineyards, fit my game a lot better than the Links at Key Biscayne. The greens were pretty open, so you could roll the ball in to the green and not have to fly it back to the pin and try and make it stop. The course played short enough that I don't remember having any problem getting to any of the holes. The greens were slower than the week before, and I made five birdies in two rounds (the last round was canceled because of lightning in the area).

I played with new Ping irons for the first time. I hit the ball over a couple of greens, which was the first indication that sometimes I was going to hit the Pings farther than I thought I would. In the wind, they acted all right, and that was one of my main concerns. I had a little problem chipping with the sand wedge, though, and didn't get quite close enough to one-putt for pars. I should have done a lot better with getting up-and-down. I think the course fit me pretty well, and I probably should have had a better tournament.

Freddie and I met a really nice couple, Helen and Sam Casey, at one of the pro-am parties. Helen kind of took us under her wing, introducing us to people and getting us a table near the dance floor. She's a sportswriter for the Naples newspaper. Her husband, Sam, is a really successful businessman and has been a member at Augusta National for something like 25 years. The next day, in the media room, Helen gave Freddie a silk picture frame so she could take a picture of our family with her on tour. Helen's written a couple notes since then and has been a really good friend.

SCORES: 73-74/147 (3 over; third round canceled)
FINISH: 40 (Tie)
EARNINGS: $2,580
YEAR-TO-DATE EARNINGS: $3,855

GTE SUNCOAST CLASSIC
TPC of Tampa Bay at Chenal, Tampa, Florida
Feb. 13 - 19, 1995

I had my best round so far on the 1995 Senior PGA Tour. I shot 69, two-under, on the first day, and I really thought I had things going my way. The second round I just didn't play very well. I was one-over after 9 holes, then I hit a ball in the water on the 10th hole and made double-bogey. I blocked a 7-iron dead right and that really surprised me, because there was no reason for that to happen. The pin was cut left and I was just trying to not miss the green left of the pin. The truth was, if I'd have just hit the ball anywhere left of the green, I'd have had a much easier situation than what I did to myself. That back nine really shot me down. Roland and I talked things over later, and we decided I had the ball positioned too far back in my stance, which was causing me to block shots to the right.

The last round, I played a little bit better, but I didn't get the ball up-and-down enough. I didn't finish with a very good tournament, even after that start. It seems like things have been downhill from there. Why, I don't know.

One funny thing that happened in Tampa was that early in the week, Freddie walked from the Ramada Inn, where we were staying, to a little strip shopping center that had a dry cleaners and a washateria. She was doing our wash when she recognized one of the tour caddies sitting around waiting on a load of clothes to dry.

"You're not supposed to be doing that," he told Freddie, motioning to the laundry. "That's part of the caddy's job."

"Thanks for letting me know," said Freddie. "I'm going to go back to the hotel and tell that to Roland."

When Freddie was in the gallery that week, a man came up to her and said that I was living out the dream of thousands of guys. "When I turn 50," he said, "I want to do just what your husband is doing."

The man said that in the meantime, though, he was looking to get a bag, and he wondered if Freddie had any suggestions where he could get one. Freddie thought that one over for a moment.

"Well, I'm not sure," she told him. "Robert's got an extra one, but it's pretty much worn out. If you need a golf bag, I believe you can probably get one in the pro shop."

The man then explained to Freddie that he was a caddy, and by "getting a bag" he meant finding a job caddying for some Senior PGA Tour player. Freddie said she felt a little bit embarrassed about that conversation.

One of the spectators at Tampa was a boy about 12 years old or so who followed me around every day. He was carrying with him a copy of the *Sports Illustrated* with an article by Austin Murphy about my first tournament at Miami. The story called "Moo Debut." At the end of the second day, he was waiting in line to get an autograph, but he kept getting pushed back as more people gathered around. So Freddie brought him up to me and told me to sign his magazine. Then she walked him out to our car and gave him one of the Dickies hats I wear. I signed that for him. Then Jay Dee Jones went over to the golf cart and pulled off the sign with my name, and I autographed that for the boy, too.

You could tell in Tampa that the *Sport Illustrated* article had really made people aware of us. Everywhere we went down there, people said hello to me and Freddie and called us by name. And some people in the gallery were mooing.

The other great thing in Tampa was that the courtesy car for players was a Cadillac with that new Northstar engine. That baby could really move. I'm not used to having so much power underneath the hood. You'd just touch the gas pedal and you'd be going 50 mighty quick.

SCORES: 69-78-75/222 (9 over)
FINISH: 58 (Tie)
EARNINGS: $1,313
YEAR-TO-DATE EARNINGS: $5,168

FHP HEALTH CARE CLASSIC
Ojai Valley Inn and Country Club, Ojai, California
Feb. 27 - March 5, 1995

Ojai was a really wonderful place, and Freddie and I had a lot of fun. The golf course was kind of neat, and really wasn't too hard. If you just hit the ball where you're supposed to hit it, you can play the course easy enough.

Getting up-and-down when I missed a green was still a little bit of a problem. That's one thing that I'm going to have to really figure out. The grasses in California were different than anything I've ever played and I had trouble with chip shots and recovery shots from the rough. It took me awhile to figure out how to chip the ball there. The greens were a little faster than in Naples, or maybe even in Tampa, but not too bad.

Once again, I didn't make enough birdies. For some reason, they have been in short supply. I don't know how many I made in two days (the third round was washed out), but it was short of my goal of three a round. I really liked the Ojai course.

Early in the week, before the tournament started, Tim Hoctor, the fellow who'd called back in January and wanted to be our host for the week, drove us down to Hollywood. Jerry had arranged several meetings with movie people, one of whom was Chuck Gordon, the big-time producer who did "Field of Dreams" and the "Die Hard" movies.

First, we met with Doug Kershner, who's with Walt Disney Studios, at one of those "in" Hollywood places where they serve about two dozen different kinds of coffee. Everything but regular and de-caf. Veronica Hamel was sitting at the table next to us, and Burt Reynolds was across the room. He was wearing sunglasses, but it was easy to tell who he was.

Before the meeting with Chuck Gordon, we looked around Universal Studios. Tim and Jerry went on a real wild simulation ride in the car from the movie "Back To The Future." Freddie and I passed on that, but they got on it and when they came back, Tim looked about two different shades of green. I'm surprised he was able to keep down his breakfast.

I hit it off with Chuck immediately. Our 15-minute meeting turned into about 90 minutes, as he put Hollywood on hold. It's like we were old friends catching up on things. Freddie said afterward she hardly got in a word, because I wouldn't shut up. That's not like either of us. It's probably the only time on record that I've out-talked Freddie.

Our last stop in Hollywood was at Paramount Pictures, where we met with Ron Smith, a producer who's a friend of Jerry's from their days growing up back in Mineral Wells. The offices at Paramount have a big trophy case with all the Academy Awards, or Oscars, Paramount has won. That was pretty impressive. We also visited the set of the hit TV show "Frasier". I got to sit in Kelsey Grammar's chair, and on the set of a new Denzel Washington movie.

Later, Tim drove us to Prime Sports Network over in Century City. One minute these TV people were running around, looking loose and disorganized, and the next minute they had me sitting down, miked up and were taping an interview that aired the next night. Those TV people can get it together in a hurry.

We watched the Prime Sports interview at the beach house of Dave and Merna Schmitt, who are friends of Tim's. They had a small dinner party for us and served Italian food, which was delicious. We appreciated their hospitality and enjoyed meeting their friends Doug Edgar, Rebecca Schmidt and Jack Rose.

Freddie and I also enjoyed staying at the Country Inn at Ventura that week, courtesy of Matt Ellison. The room had its own kitchenette, with a refrigerator and microwave. Freddie and I went down to the grocery store early in the week and stocked up on sandwich fixings and snacks. That way, we never had to leave the room for meals, or pay those Los Angeles prices to eat out.

Matt Ellison grew up in the same area as Corey Pavin, and a few weeks earlier he'd gone over to the Nissan Los Angeles Open at Riviera Country Club to see his old friend. Corey saw him coming up and said, "Matt, I heard you won a $50,000 BMW the other day with a hole-in-one."

Matt confirmed the story was true.

"Well," said Corey. "Touch me on the shoulder and give me some good luck."

So Matt touched Corey on the shoulder and, sure enough, Corey won the Los Angeles Open for the second straight year.

When I heard that story, I asked Matt to touch me on the shoulder, which he was happy to do. Only things didn't work out quite the same way for me in Los Angeles as they did for Corey Pavin.

SCORES: 71-72/143 (3 over; third round rained out)
FINISH: 49 (Tie)
EARNINGS: $1,913
YEAR-TO-DATE EARNINGS: $7,081

SBC PRESENTS THE DOMINION SENIORS
The Dominion Country Club, San Antonio, Texas
March 6 - 12, 1995

Although conditions in San Antonio were windy and cold, there really weren't any problems on the course. For the first time on Tour, I struggled hitting my driver. I had been driving the ball well in all the earlier tournaments. At The Dominion, I was trying to use an Odyssey driver, but I kept hitting the ball to the right. I let that one club hurt me too much. When I missed a green, I wasn't able to hit the soft chip I needed to get the ball up-and-down. The greens were plenty quick, and together with the undulation, they were a bit of a problem to play. Again, the birdies weren't there. Like on one par-5, I had a 5-iron to the green and I just flat missed the shot. One thing you simply must do is take advantage of the opportunities when they're there. I didn't.

The highlight of the week was being invited to take part in the Merrill Lynch Shoot-Out for the first time. I hung in there pretty well, too, making a couple clutch par putts to keep going. At the end, it came down to me and Dave Eichelberger. On the last hole, I hit my approach shot into the water, which handed him first place. Second place paid $3,000 (I made a $100 bonus for sinking a 34-foot birdie putt on the eighth hole), which was more than I made in the tournament itself. I sure would like the chance to play in a few more of those Shoot-Outs, but I need to earn my way in.

San Antonio was a busy week for us. We made an appearance at Tom Benson Chevrolet, where we did some meeting and greeting with the dealership's customers and sales staff. We also made an appearance at the Texas Sports Bar in the Hilton by the San Antonio Airport. That was fun, although I don't believe I threatened David Robinson on the popularity charts.

I also had a meeting with Dr. Deborah Graham, a sports psychologist who lives in Boerne, Texas, not far from San Antonio. Dr. Graham has worked with Dave Stockton and a lot of the guys on the tour. She also helped the 1991 U.S. Ryder Cup team get mentally geared up for its big win, when America reclaimed the Cup.

Dr. Graham said she thought I probably was being pulled in too many directions—fans, sponsors, media and so on—to play my best golf. She advised me I'd better learn how to say "no." She also said I needed to be more tough-minded about my own situation and less tender-minded about other players. It's true. When my opponents are having problems, I tend to sympathize with what's happening to them.

Freddie decided to practice some psychology, too. She told Jimmy Burch of the *Fort Worth Star-Telegram,* who was down covering the tournament, that I needed to have "more intensity" and show some of the "ruthlessness" of the other competitors. "You can see the killer instinct in their eyes," Freddie said.

Man, I don't know about being ruthless. But I am working on getting tougher mentally. I know that sometimes in the past, when I've made a birdie, for some reason I have a letdown on the next hole. I get careless and let that stroke slip away. I need to string a bunch of them. Maybe I need to go back to my old method of trying to divide a course in three-hole segments and shooting for one birdie in each segments.

Freddie and I had a lot of family and friends following us at The Dominion. My daughter, Barbee, and her husband, Keith Walker, came down from Fort Worth. My nephew, Scott Moreland, brought his family up from Corpus Christi. Freddie's daughter, Lisa Rose; son-in-law, H.L. Rose; and grandchildren Tiffany Hall, Melissa Wilson and Trina Smith were also part of the group. So was Trina's boyfriend, Orlando Cantu.

Lisa was a real trooper that week. While we were in Ojai the week before, they had some wintery weather back in North Texas. Lisa had gone to the farm early one morning to feed the cows, and she slipped on a patch of ice and broke her ankle in two places.

That didn't keep her from coming to San Antonio, though. She was in a wheelchair, and H.L. had to push her around every day, so I'm sure that was real hard on both of them. But we sure thank them for being there as part of the Moo Crew.

San Antonio was the first stop where the black-and-white, Holstein-patterned "Moo Crew" hats were available in the pro shop. By the time Freddie's grandkids went to get some, there'd been a run on them and they were sold out. We got some for them, later.

My son, Robert III, couldn't get down to San Antonio because of his class schedule at DeVry Institute of Technology in Irving, where he's studying electronics. But several friends from Azle, including Johnny Admire, Randy Admire, Bobby Boyd, Bill Ortego,

Scott Allred, and John Rangle were in the gallery. So were some of my buddies from Mineral Wells, including Jerry Ray, George Gault, John Gault, Tim Blasor, Ike Mercer, Brian Petty and Charles Gatlin.

On their way home from San Antonio, Jerry Hamilton, Jerry Ray and Charles Gatlin were pulled over by a Texas Highway Patrolman near the town of Hico. The officer asked them what the rush was, and they said they were still pumped up from watching me play in the tournament.

It so happened the patrolman was a golfer and a Moo Crew supporter, and he wanted to know all about how I had played. He let them off without a speeding ticket, just because they were Robert Landers' fans.

I'm glad I was able to help someone that week. I didn't do all that much to help myself.

SCORES: 76-71-78/225 (9 over)

FINISH: 64 (Tie)

EARNINGS: $878

YEAR-TO-DATE EARNINGS: $7,959

TOSHIBA SENIOR CLASSIC
Mesa Verde Country Club, Costa Mesa, California
March 13 - 19, 1995

Costa Mesa was the first tournament where the fairways were nice and tight. Driving was at premium as far as playing the golf course. I was still struggling with the tee shots, trying both Odyssey and Pro-Gear drivers. I was having to play from places where I just couldn't play from.

The greens were poa annua and were difficult for me to play. I had trouble hitting them in regulation, and when I did, it was like putting on a rub board. I let a couple putts get away from me. I made too many bogies. I made eight birdies in that tournament, my best so far, but I couldn't cover up all the mistakes I was making.

One of the worst mistakes was on the first hole. I topped my tee shot and it only went about 150 or 160 yards. There probably wasn't any guy in the gallery that didn't immediately think he could beat me. To make things worse, I made a poor club choice on the second shot. Instead of laying up from the rough with a medium iron, or even a short iron, I tried to hit a 5-wood from a downhill lie. I sculled that shot into the water and made a double-bogey. That's what I mean when I say I haven't been thinking too well on the golf course. Either I don't have a plan, or I have a bad plan.

I met with Bob Downey of Lectronic Kaddy, who demonstrated his product. A remote-controlled caddy is a great idea and it's perfect for me, because when I play golf I prefer walking to riding in a cart. Many serious golfers do.

The most fun moment of the week came on Saturday, when Chi Chi Rodriguez pulled Freddie inside the ropes on the 18th fairway and told us to walk up to the green together, holding hands. Everyone gave us a big ovation, which made us feel great.

SCORES: 75-73-73/221 (11 over)
FINISH: 68 (Tie)
EARNINGS: $728
EARNINGS YEAR-TO-DATE: $8,687

THE TRADITION PRESENTED BY SCOTTS
Golf Club at Desert Mountain, Scottsdale, Arizona
March 27 - April 2, 1995

I did all right the first couple of days at Desert Mountain. I hit my tee shots well, using a Chicago Classic driver, and hit a fair number of greens. The greens were fast and hard. I was beginning to get the hang of hitting the soft, high chips I need around the greens, but I just couldn't putt those greens. They were too fast for me.

The last day on the last nine I was trying to hit the driver way too hard. I ended up hitting it in the desert three times in the last 10 holes. That just killed me. I probably shot at least six shots higher in the last round—an ugly 82—than I should have, mainly because of mistakes with the driver.

I hit the ball a lot farther than I had been with the Ping irons. I went to the Ping factory in Phoenix and got them reset, because I was having a problem hitting the ball too far. Either the shots wouldn't hold, or the bounce would be funny. Anyway, I had an extremely difficult time trying to manage my game, and I only made two birdies in four rounds, which just isn't going to work. Someday, I hope to do a lot better job of it.

One of the highlights of the week was going to the Phoenix Greyhound Park, a beautiful facility near the airport. We went with Jerry and Jay Dee Jones, and Jay Dee's girlfriend, Tracey Wilson. They were doing a pretty good job picking winners with trifectas and quinellas, but Freddie and I were shooting blanks. Freddie said I'd better keep her away from the slot machines when we go to Las Vegas in a few weeks. I think she's probably right. At the track that night, we ran into Herman Mitchell, who's Lee Trevino's caddy. Herman and some friends of his were seated at a table not far from the betting windows. I hope they had better luck at the track than we did.

Later that same week, Herman was admitted to a hospital in Scottsdale with a congestive heart problem. We sure hope he's doing better. And Freddie and I have said a prayer for Tommy Aycock, the Senior PGA Tour player from Texas, who has been diagnosed with cancer and has been undergoing treatment.

Chi Chi Rodriguez played a big role in the days leading up to, and including, Phoenix. He's always been extra nice to me since I started on tour. In fact, the Friday before we were supposed to go to Arizona, while I was at home in Azle, he called and told me and Freddie to fly down to Houston the next day. He had a friend who wanted to meet me. Chi Chi said we could go on to Phoenix from Houston on his private plane.

We flew to Houston on Saturday morning on American Eagle and met up with Chi Chi. We played golf with his friend, Frank Wade, at Lochnivar, a real high-dollar private club. Since Lochnivar doesn't allow women members or guests, Freddie spent the day with Mrs. Wade at their beautiful new home. Freddie told me later it was another mansion, like Raymond Floyd's.

Frank, who's the head of his own oil company, F.W. Oil, said that day he'd been interested in a sponsorship arrangement. I told him I'd talk to Jerry, and we'd try to work something out. As it turned out, we were able to make a deal a couple weeks later.

While we were down in Houston, I asked Chi Chi, who's one of world's best bunker players, for a little help with my sand shots. "What do you want to know?" he asked, as I was hitting some shots in the practice area at Lochnivar.

"I need some help with bunker shots from 30 or 60 yards," I told him.

"Forget it, Robert," said Chi Chi. "Nobody can hit those shots." He then showed me how to weaken my right hand to produce a higher, softer explosion shot with a little more bite.

Jerry told me to be sure to ask Chi Chi what time we would be getting to Phoenix. Jerry needed to know so he could call out there and guarantee our reservation for late arrival, if need be. So I asked Chi Chi what time we were headed west.

"Whenever we want to," Chi Chi responded. "I own the plane."

We flew out to Phoenix late Saturday night. There was some confusion when we got to the hotel in Scottsdale, because it turned out Jerry had been unable to make reservations for Freddie and me. The place had no vacancies. But here came Chi Chi to the rescue. He had three rooms reserved in his own name, and he quickly did some shuffling around of his crowd, and we wound up with a room.

"And I tell you what, Robert," said Chi Chi. "Your room for tonight and tomorrow night is on me. I'm picking up the tab for you and Freddie." Which he did.

In one of the rounds in the Tradition, I was paired with Bob Brue. He's a clever, funny man, a guy who's known for saying things like "Why do people park on driveways and drive on parkways?" and "Why are there interstate highways in Hawaii?"

He was facing a real delicate pitch shot on one hole and right before he hit, he looked over at the gallery and asked, "What kind of odds will you give me on this shot?"

"Ten to one," hollered Jay Dee Jones.

Brue addressed his ball for a moment, then turned back around to look at Jay Dee. "Tell you what," said Bob, "give me $500 that I don't make it."

SCORES: 79-76-75-82/312 (24 Over)

FINISH: 70

EARNINGS: $880

YEAR-TO-DATE EARNINGS: $9,567

LAS VEGAS SENIOR CLASSIC

TPC at Summerlin, Las Vegas, Nevada

April 24 - 30, 1995

I used the new Adams Assault irons for the first time in competition and they worked great. In the first round, for example, I hit at seven or eight irons to 10 feet or less. I made three birdies, but left several good chances on the table. The breaks weren't the best, either. On the par-5 ninth hole, for example, I hit a good looking second shot on to the green. I thought I'd have probably 20 feet for eagle, but the ball took a weird bounce and kicked into a trap. I hit the bunker shot over the green, chipped short, missed the putt and made six. I turned a possible eagle and sure birdie into a sorry bogey.

The second round I shot myself right out of the tournament with a fat, ugly 9 on the sixth hole. I can't remember the last time I shot a number that high. I must have gone to sleep, because I topped my 3-wood tee shot into the desert for starters. Then things got really bad. I tried to play back to the fairway, but hit a fat 9-iron that stayed in the desert. I had to take an unplayable lie, go back to the front tee and play my fourth shot. I hit a solid 5-wood to 97 yards short of the green. From there, my fifth shot was a sand wedge that hit the green, then spun back down a slope and rolled 40 yards from the pin.

I tried lobbing the sixth shot with a sand wedge, but the ball hit into the bank and rolled back. The same exact thing happened on the seventh shot. It's like I was playing putt-putt golf, and I couldn't get the ball up the anthill on the 18th hole. On the third pitch shot with the sand wedge, number eight overall, I hit the ball all the way to the hole, and it stopped 15 feet past. I made the putt coming back to stay out of double figures.

I wasn't completely sure about my score. I thought I might have made a ten. The scorer in our group thought I made an eight. On the next hole, I had to get Tom Weiskopf, my playing partner, to help me add up the strokes. I had to be sure, because I didn't want to write down the wrong score, sign an incorrect scorecard and get disqualified.

I think playing with a great champion like Tom Weiskopf was a valuable experience. He probably didn't have that much better a ballstriking round than I did, although he hits the ball a whole lot farther. But he sure knows how to manage his game and get around the course. His scorecard showed 69—ten shots lower than mine. I guess playing with me didn't hurt his game any.

The final round, I played with Billy Casper. He was friendly, though we didn't talk too much. He put on a clinic in the bunkers, hitting everything to tap-in range. I didn't make a single birdie in the final round, as the greens, once again, ate my lunch.

Other than the golf, we had an exciting week. I got to visit with my buddy Keith Flatt, who caddied for me in a practice round before Roland arrived. Keith gave me some local knowledge on the TPC-Summerlin course. Tommy Wilson, a friend of Jerry's, gave us the use of a limousine while we were town. That was a really nice ride to and from the golf course.

Our hotel room at Caesar's Palace, which Jay Dee Jones arranged through the casino, was something real swanky. It had a round bed, a jacuzzi and plenty of mirrors. We were about eight floors up or so, which gave us a great view of The Strip. Not that we ever got out and walked around any. Freddie's back was hurting, and I did enough walking on the golf course.

As Freddie kept insisting, and I agreed, all this ritzy business just wasn't us. For example, we had to spend more money for one meal, which was more like a snack, really, than we are used to paying for one night's stay in a hotel.

Freddie's luck at the casino wasn't so hot, either. She tried the nickel slots (not for long), then the quarter slots, then the dollar slots. Nothing was hitting. She went through her daily limit of $34 right quick. I played just a little on the quarter slots, and nothing happened. I did have five 7s come up on one spin, but I only had one quarter in there, not the five you needed for the big payoff.

On Saturday night, Jerry and Kathy Hamilton were playing roulette in the casino with Bonnie Ray, who's Jerry Ray's wife. They all talked me into playing a little. I lost a spin or two, then put $2 on number "9"—because of that horrible number I'd made on the golf course. I figure it had to mean something. Wouldn't you know it, that little number came up on the very next spin, and I won $70. The others stayed around playing for awhile, hitting some numbers right on the nose and getting several hundred dollars ahead. Me, I took my $70 and went to bed.

One other memorable thing was that in the pro-am on Thursday, the wind was blowing at least 45 mph. I haven't played in such conditions in a long time, if ever. You could place your ball on the greens and it would start rocking before you could even putt. On one hole, I had a three-footer that the wind blew to within a couple inches of the hole. I mean, it almost went in without a stroke. Now that could help a fellow's putting statistics.

SCORES: 73-79-78
FINISH: 55
EARNINGS: $2,500
YEAR-TO-DATE EARNINGS: $12,067

PAINE WEBBER INVITATIONAL
TPC at Piper Glen, Charlotte, North Carolina
May 1 - May 7, 1995

The course had a lot of mounds and a lot of slope and really didn't fit my game all that well. I got off to another poor start, a six-over 78, with three penalty strokes for balls in the hazard. I was trying a new Calloway Big Bertha driver and blocked a few shots to the right. I rallied a bit in the second round with a 73, which should have been about a 67. I missed three makeable birdie putts and three short putts for par. I closed with a 74.

I was hitting the ball better than I had in weeks. On Saturday, for example, I must have hit eight approach shots to within 10 or 12 feet. Hobo, who's the caddy for Don Massengale, my playing partner that day, told Jerry Hamilton, "Your guy is a shotmaker. I've never seen anyone hit it so close so much. He should be winning out here, or doing better than he has been." Of course, Hobo didn't make any comment about my putting.

Other than the first day, I started driving the ball really well at Charlotte. I used a 46-inch Adams Air Assault and got some consistency going. Of all the drivers I've tried in the past two months, the Adams is the longest and definitely the most accurate. I plan to keep it in the bag.

The Adams equipment was the talk of the locker room. Rocky Thompson said he's been using an Adams Air Assault 10.5 degree driver as his 3-wood. Lee Trevino told me he's using an Adams 3-wood and hitting it great. Lee also asked me to make an appearance with him at Chicago later this summer. That outing will pay $5,000, so I didn't hesitate in accepting.

Before the Paine Webber tournament started, I joined several of the guys at an inner-city golf clinic. Charlie Sifford, Walt Morgan, Bruce Crampton, Bruce Summerhays and I went down to South Side Park in Charlotte and put on a program for kids. That's the kind of thing I really enjoy doing.

The guy organizing the event was James Black, who played on the PGA Tour for awhile in the 1960s. One of the caddies told me that in Jim's very first tournament, the 1964 Los Angeles Open, he shot 67 on the first day and had the lead.

The players were curious about this newcomer. "Just who is this Jim Black?" someone asked the next morning on the practice tee.

"I don't know," replied Dow Finsterwald, the winner of the Los Angeles Open in 1960. "But one thing I do know is that he beat the hell out of me."

In the Wednesday pro-am, I had a bit of a problem. On the third green, when I reached down to mark my ball, the zipper on my pants blew out. I got it fixed, but a couple holes later, the same thing happened. Then on the eighth hole, a short par-3, just as I hit my pitching wedge, the zipper exploded again. While the guys in my pro-am group were watching the flight of the ball to the green, I was busy tending to business. Maybe I need to ease up on the Waffle House hash browns. Or maybe I need to wear my Harbor One golf pants from Dickies. That would eliminate the problem.

Freddie and I stayed in Gastonia, North Carolina, at the home of Jess and Phyllis Osborn. The Osborns, who are good friends with one of Jerry's pals from home, J.W. Blue, were really nice people, and so were their neighbors, Chuck and Lavon Ramsey. The Ramseys loaned us their late model Ford pickup truck, which has the name of Chuck's company, Carolina Custom Windows, painted on the doors. It really stood out in the parking lot at Piper Glen, sitting next to all those courtesy Cadillacs.

This was our first time to accept someone's offer to put us up, mainly because we hate to impose on anyone. We sure enjoyed the good company and conversation, however, so maybe we were a bit hasty when we said "No" to Tim Hoctor.

The big news of the week was that on Friday, Freddie decided to return to Texas and get some rest. She was still jet-lagged from the trip to Las Vegas and not feeling very well. We decided she'd be better off in Azle for a week, taking things easy at the farm, while I headed to the Cadillac NFL Golf Classic in New Jersey.

On May 15, Orville Moody, Bob Charles and I were scheduled to fly down to Texas to play in the Eisenhower Pro-Am at Willow Brook Country Club in Tyler. A bunch of guys from the PGA Tour like Tom Kite, Mark Brooks, Hal Sutton and Brian Henninger, and some of the women pros, like Annika Sorenstam, would be there. Freddie and I made plans to hook up at Dallas/Fort Worth International Airport that night, and then we'll fly to Philadelphia for the Bell Atlantic Classic.

With Freddie gone, I was feeling a little bit lonesome the last three nights in Charlotte. Helping to cheer me up was the Osborns' dog, a Pomeranian named Missy. Missy, who is a little beige ball of fluff, could do all sorts of tricks. She could beg, shake hands and roll over. She could also play dead, but first you had to shoot her with your finger and say "Bang!"

When I get home this fall, maybe I'll try to teach a few dog tricks to Oleo. Assuming Oleo's still around.

SCORES: 78-73-74

FINISH: 61T

EARNINGS: $1,320

EARNINGS YEAR-TO-DATE: $13,387

You can take one look at my statistics over the first couple months (through the Paine Webber Invitational) and see the problem. First, my scoring average was 75.12, which is the kind of figure that earns you a one-way ticket back to the qualifying tournament. That average has to drop over the summer months.

Breaking down the stats a little, I was averaging 243 yards in driving distance—which is too short (68th on tour). I've giving up about 20 yards, or two clubs, a hole to the stronger players. That usually catches up with you over 18 holes or, especially, 54 holes. I have to figure out how to get more distance without losing any accuracy.

Driving accuracy is the one stat where I'm doing pretty well. Again, through Charlotte, I was hitting 72 percent of the fairways.

That was 21st best on tour. In the total driving category, ranked a respectable 49th overall.

My iron play is what blows my mind. It's been a big disappointment. Despite hitting 72 percent of the fairways, I was hitting only 55 percent of the greens in regulation. That ranked near the bottom (73rd) and it's hard to figure out why. I've always been good with those clubs—even the burned ones. I suppose it hasn't helped me all that much that I've tried a lot of different equipment in the first couple of months of the tour. I probably should stick to one set, for better or worse.

My sand play has been decent. I was getting up-and-down from the bunkers 42.9 percent of the time, which ranked 57th. The other big bugaboo, though, was putting. I'd been taking 30.77 putts per round, which ranked 78th. I need to be somewhere in the high 20s in putts per round to have a chance out here.

Everyone said that the hardest adjustment for me would be getting a feel for the speed of the greens. They were right. The municipal courses I'm accustomed to playing are just a bit faster than the slow shag carpet in our living room. Greens on the Senior PGA Tour, by contrast, all seem pretty dang slick. I'm working hard at smoothing out my putting stroke, and Roland and I are spending more time trying to read those devils. We have to try something.

I look at my stats and see areas where I need immediate improvement. Driving distance, approach-shot accuracy and putting, to name the most obvious three. You have to understand, though, that golf is the sort of game that can turn around for you in a flash. You just have to be patient. You have to trust yourself and your swing. You can't be thinking any negative thoughts, no matter how much you may be struggling, because then negative things will happen. You have to keep a positive attitude and approach.

That's one of the thing I admire so much about Chi Chi Rodriguez. He's always positive. He could be five-over for a round,—well, maybe not five-over, but over-par—and you'd never know it by his actions or what he had to say. He'd still be smiling, joking and cheering everybody up.

I'm hoping the new Adams Golf equipment I've been using the past few weeks—woods and irons—brings me some consistency. If I can settle the equipment issue, and find a putter that will make a few putts, I'm still confident that I'll give a good accounting of myself. Especially in the summer months, when I've always played my best golf.

Chapter Twelve

WHERE DO WE
GO FROM HERE?

As I've said several times already, Freddie and I have been having the time of our lives on the 1995 Senior PGA Tour. In a way, though, we probably feel a lot like kids at their first carnival. There's just so much excitement, so many things happening all around, that these new sights, sounds and experiences have us feeling overwhelmed.

These first few months, I've probably have had the same "big eyes" that a kid gets when he or she sees a ferris wheel, roller coaster or merry-go-round for the first time, or hears the noise, or smells the cotton candy, along the midway. I know I need to get over my wide-eyed wonder and narrow the focus down to one thing: playing good golf.

That may not be quite as easy as it sounds. The changes to our lifestyle have been extreme. Before we went to Tampa last November, we probably hadn't stayed in a motel since we went to the Oklahoma Open in 1987. We probably hadn't gone out to eat dinner since we went to Long John Silver's on our wedding day in 1990. I know for sure I hadn't been on an airplane since flying back east for the Sunnehanna Amateur in 1981.

Now we've landed smack dab in the fast lane, traveling to a new city each week, seeing new golf courses and meeting new people. This new schedule of ours is all about airline reservations, packing suitcases, checking into hotels, driving courtesy cars or rental cars around in strange cities, valet parking, pro-am parties, signing autographs, giving interviews, being on TV and so forth. It's all about meeting with book publishers, movie makers, lawyers, agents and sales representatives from this golf company or that. It's about getting phone calls at all hours from someone wanting a piece of my time. And yes, it's about receiving faxes.

Sometimes Freddie and I feel like we're visiting a different planet than the one we've lived on all our lives.

Is all this hustle and bustle harmful to my golf game? Maybe, maybe not. I can't really say for sure, but in the first four months of the 1995 tour, I know that I haven't been playing golf like my old self.

For some reason, I haven't been approaching the game with the same tunnel-vision and carefully thought-out strategy that I had for so many years playing in Fort Worth. Perhaps part of the explanation could have to do with unfamiliarity with all the things around me. I may be going through what some people call "culture shock." Freddie and I may be completely out of our comfort zone.

I'm hoping that, as the weeks go by, I'll grow more accustomed to the travel and more accustomed to all the things that happen on tour that are unrelated to golf. I hope to start taking everything in stride, like the veterans out here do. That alone should help me settle down some.

Freddie and I have been deeply moved by all the support golf fans have shown. How can you not be touched, when a couple like Jack and Donna Peyton of Fort Lauderdale decides to celebrate their 38th wedding anniversary by following me around at Key Biscayne? Seems Jack was a dairy farmer back in his home state of Kentucky, and he looked upon me and Freddie as kindred souls.

How can you not be touched when a nice man in Dallas named Clay Killion sends us a card for Easter and encloses a check for $5, so we can have a meal at McDonald's?

How can you not be touched when friends you haven't seen in 30 years—Denny and Barbara Anderson, who I knew when I was attending TCU—show up out of the blue at San Antonio? We'd really like to have more time to visit with the Andersons or the Peytons or Mr. Killion, or any other Moo Crew member that becomes, however briefly, a part of our lives.

Some readers may be wondering about Freddie's and my future, and we appreciate your concern. Thanks to all the endorsement deals Jerry Hamilton's helped line up for us, we should have plenty of money to cover the expenses associated with traveling around the country to play in 30-something golf tournaments this year.

We should also have enough money left over to be able to pay off our home mortgage. And, who knows, maybe even buy that new tractor we've been needing so badly for the farm.

I'm hoping that, when all is said and done, Freddie and I are not put in the position where we have to go back and get minimum-wage jobs, like before. One of my prime goals would be that Freddie doesn't ever have to go back to work, period. If she wants to, fine. That's her choice. Wanting to work and having to work, however, are two different things altogether.

I DON'T LOK AT THE 1995 SENIOR PGA TOUR LIKE THIS IS SOME SORT OF MAKE-OR-BREAK DEAL.

With the endorsement money covering our expenses, everything I make in tournament competition should go right into our savings account. That might be $35,000—at the rate I've started out the year—or it could be $350,000, if I get hot and have a good stretch of tournaments. That money will become our nest egg for whatever happens next.

I don't look at the 1995 Senior PGA Tour like this is some sort of make-or-break deal. I think you put too much pressure on yourself that way. Instead of worrying about the money, I just want to get to where I'm playing the kind of golf I know I can play. Right now, I'm not even close to that level.

I figure that if I place an emphasis on playing good golf, the money will surely follow. On the other hand, if I try to make money my main focus, good golf won't necessarily follow.

What's ahead for the farmers from Azle? Without having a crystal ball, that's pretty difficult to say. Freddie and I have been so busy week to week, we really haven't given the future that much thought.

One thing's for certain: Because I've worked so long and so hard just to reach this level in golf, there's no way I'm walking away from the game. Competitive golf will be in my future more than it's been in my past.

If I keep my Senior PGA Tour card for next year, great. To do that, I will have to finish in the top 31 money winners for 1995, which will probably take at least $300,000 in official earnings. To reach that target, I obviously will need to start having a series of top five or top ten finishes. A tournament win or two along the way wouldn't hurt, either.

If I don't make the top 31, and don't keep my card, I'll toss my Dickies hat back into the Senior PGA Tour qualifying for 1996. I have a good feel for the TPC course at Tampa Bay, and good memories from last November's tournament. I could conceivably go back down there and regain my playing status for 1996.

On the other hand, if I don't keep my Senior PGA Tour playing privileges, or don't re-qualify for the tour, I will still continue to compete in golf in 1996. Some of the Senior PGA Tour stops might extend me a sponsor's invitation, if they think I'm deserving. There's also a Senior Series tour, which has some real good players and pretty good purses, now active for much of the year. And there's the Lone Star Tour right here in Texas.

As the Baby Boom generation begins reaching the big Five-O, as it's starting to do, it stands to reason that increased attention will be paid to senior golf. That will create more opportunities for old guys like me.

If I'm not out playing the Senior PGA Tour or Senior Series in 1996, there's a possibility I might be working in the golf business somewhere close to home. Who knows, maybe at Cross Timbers in Azle or maybe at a golf course somewhere around Fort Worth. I've always wanted to work in golf but never did, mainly because I had a secure job at Mitchell's and would never have considered taking the risk of starting a new career. Now, though, I'm in a position to consider that alternative.

As much as I enjoy working in the fresh air and pushing around dirt, maybe I'll hire out to my old friend Phil Lumsden and help him build his second 18-hole golf course down at Sugar Tree in Dennis, Texas. Something like that would be rewarding, as well as a lot of fun.

One way or the other, I definitely plan to stay active in golf. I want to give back to the game as much as I possibly can. And I will continue to introduce kids to golf, whether as a volunteer golf coach at some high school, or just someone who gives junior clinics or teaches on the driving range. That's one priority that will never change.

Kids need a little something to shoot for in their lives. You can't just turn them loose in the streets. I like to talk to kids about golf, and do my best to help them understand the value of pursuing any sport with total commitment. The discipline you get from training and competing spills over into all aspects of your life. Sports like golf can make you a better person.

I used to have a good friend in Azle named Norman Ott, who was a police officer and a member of Sertoma. I had a world of respect for Norman, and that respect was built on the work he did with kids—whether teaching them at school about drug awareness or holding classes in the community about gun safety. I always considered him to be a shining example of the good things life has to offer.

That is how I would like to be regarded some day. I would want people to feel about me the same way I feel about Norman Ott. I would like people to think of me not as a good golfer, but as a good person.

Sometimes I wonder why I have dedicated so much of my life to playing golf. As I quickly discovered, golf is a life consuming process. To be successful at it takes every spare minute you've got.

I sometimes think about other people and some of their life-consuming projects—whether it's raising their children or taking care of their invalid parents. I know you can't really put golf in the same category as those things, or give it the same importance. But I do know golf takes the same kind of dedication and effort.

I guess I chose to devote myself to the game because I discovered golf represents the ultimate challenge of all the skills a person can muster: mental, physical and emotional. Golf requires you to accept failure and control your anger. Golf requires you to remain constant and level-headed, especially when you're faced with anxiety and fear. Golf requires you to keep your emotional state on an even keel.

A friend of mine once told me, "Anyone who would cheat in golf would cheat in life." Obviously, he was talking about cheating your fellow man. I don't look at golf quite in that same way—cheating to beat your opponent—because you're not playing anyone except yourself. Your opponent is you.

I do look at golf, however, as if it might be the last frontier between me and the Lord. That's why I try to be considerate, kind and helpful to anyone I meet on a golf course. Even if I'm trying like heck to beat them out for first prize.

Golf to me represents sport in its purest form. You have to be able to stand on your own two feet, without relying on anyone else. The rules are the same for everyone, so your honor, character and integrity are put to a test every time you tee it up. If you play the game properly, you can tell what you're made of, deep down inside.

My friend John Patty once told me that when he was in high school, playing golf matches, he would have to look away when his opponent was attempting an important putt. The reason he looked away was so that he wouldn't be tempted to wish that the putt would be missed. I believe that if someone could carry this attitude to the golf course, and throughout his or her life, that person's integrity would show through clearly to others.

I know a lot of people who follow the Senior PGA Tour are in my corner, pulling for me as the ultimate underdog. Freddie and I can feel the good vibrations everywhere we go on tour. Maybe I can do something one day soon to justify all the fans' support. Maybe I can give the gallery a reason to roar.

Or maybe I've already had my brief moment of glory, my one shot of fame. The sports books are full of stories about people who were heroes one day and gone practically the next. People like Karl Spooner, or Mark "The Bird" Fydrich or Buster Douglas.

No matter what happens, I hope that I never set foot on a golf course without taking time to appreciate all its natural beauty. To listen to the movement of the tree limbs and feel the wind blowing against my face. To hear birds singing or animals playing. To see flowers in bloom, or smell freshly cut fairways. I hope that I never overlook, or take for granted, God's magnificent creation in the great outdoors.

Freddie and I will be out on the Senior PGA Tour, for sure, for the rest of 1995. We hope to meet you all, and get to shake your hand. If you make it out to one of the tournaments, be sure to come by and give us a moo.

Chapter Thirteen

DO-IT-YOURSELF
GOLF GUIDE

I've never had a golf lesson in my life. I've never had my golf swing videotaped and analyzed. I don't read tips in golf magazines. I've never read a golf instruction book—not Ben Hogan's or David Leadbetter's.

What I have done is learn the game of golf from the ground up. At Rockwood Park, Carswell AFB and at city parks in Fort Worth and Azle, I taught myself to play by trial-and-error. Or, as I like to say, mostly by error.

I am probably what more golfers should be—self-made and self-sufficient. That is not to say you shouldn't ever see a PGA or LPGA teaching pro. You probably would benefit from having one introduce you to the basic fundamentals. It's just that once you get started in golf, I think you should learn the game by yourself.

After all, the only person who can hit the ball is you. When you get in a tight situation, there's no substitute who can come running in off the bench and bail you out. You have to rely on yourself.

One thing that would help any golfer would be a grasp of why things happen in golf. Whenever I would mis-hit a shot, I always took the time to figure out why. What I realized is that, basically, every golf shot you hit is the result of cause and effect. For example, if you top a ball (effect), you've likely pulled up on the shot (cause). If you slice a ball (effect), your clubhead path is probably too much inside going back (cause), or your weight shift is poor (cause), both of which encourage an out-to-in path coming back to the ball. That puts sidespin on the ball and causes it to fly left-to-right, sometimes in exaggerated fashion. If you pop up the shot (effect), your swing plane is probably way too steep (cause). So turn your body more and lift the club less.

If you use this kind of common sense approach to golf, you'll find yourself hitting better shots. Why? Because you'll understand the source of any problem and have some idea how to correct it.

As I've mentioned several times already—mainly because it's so critical to playing good golf—I learned to manage my way around a golf course. I figured out where the trouble areas were and avoided them at all costs.

I also developed a scoring system to identify my weaknesses, so I would know where to concentrate my practice time. I'll share that system later in this chapter, in hopes that my method can offer better ways for handling the game.

How did I pull off this amazing feat of making the 1995 Senior PGA Tour, besides by hitting hundreds of thousands of practice balls? I prepared myself for success in golf. Beginning in the early 1970s, I adopted the mental approach of trying hard on every shot and playing the ball down. I also had the discipline not to be too hard on myself, or beat myself up, whenever I hit a poor shot.

I can't tell you how frequently I see amateur players getting really down on themselves because they've made mistakes. That's the wrong attitude to have, because no matter who you are, you'll make mistakes in golf.

It's a game of mistakes. On the professional level, it's a game of managing those mistakes. One problem I've been having at the early stops on the 1995 Senior PGA Tour is making poor decisions and putting myself in jail too often, where I can't recover from my mistakes. The culprit has been poor decision-making, and course management, as much as bad execution.

I'd like to share a few thoughts about what I've learned about the golf swing and playing golf. I hope it will encourage some readers, or inspire them to know that if I can teach myself to play good golf consistently, so can they. Keep in mind, I had no obvious talent as an athlete. College recruiters weren't knocking at my door, begging for my services. I was just your average guy with your average athletic ability. The difference was I committed everything I had to golf.

I also developed an immediate, intense love for the game—probably because it fit with my natural liking for the outdoors. I set performance goals and practiced with a purpose. I think anyone who puts his or her heart and soul into golf can see rapid improvement, too.

THE GOLF SWING

If I were going to teach someone how to play golf, I'd probably want to work with either an adult, who's never played, or a young person just starting out. The reason I say that is I've found, through the years, that I have a much easier time relating to someone like that, someone who doesn't think that he or she already has all the answers.

It's funny, but you meet a lot of people in golf who consider themselves to be experts on the golf swing, and yet they can hardly hit the ball out of their own shadow.

Some of the ideas about the golf swing I've developed are based on things I've tried through the years. My methods might go against the grain of what someone else thinks, or the way some famous golf instructors teach, but they work for me.

GRIP

The first thing I would teach anyone would be how to put their left, or front, hand on the golf club, so that the club is held primarily with the last three fingers and not in the palm.

*

IF I WERE GOING TO TEACH SOMEONE HOW TO PLAY GOLF, I'D PROBABLY WANT TO WORK WITH EITHER AN ADULT, WHO'S NEVER PLAYED, OR A YOUNG PERSON JUST STARTING OUT.

I use an interlocking grip, where the little finger of the right hand interlocks between the little finger and ring finger of the left hand. That doesn't mean, necessarily, that I would teach someone that grip. I would give them the choice between the interlocking, overlapping or baseball grip—whichever feels the most comfortable to them.

My grip has evolved from years and years of playing. Nobody ever showed me another way to hold the club. I realize now that the one difference between my grip and many other pros' is that the club goes diagonally across my right hand. That's pretty unusual, because, generally, it's taught that you should keep the club up in the fingers of the right hand.

Once you have the clubhead on the ground, with your left hand on the club to where the angle of shaft and your left arm are pretty much on a straight line, with the hands ahead of the clubhead, then your right hand simply reaches down and underneath and fits on the club.

The tendency in the grip is for everybody to have too strong a right hand, that is, they carry the right hand too much underneath the club. Trying to get the right hand in a bit of a weaker position, up on top of the club, is pretty difficult to do. It's not the most natural feeling, but it's important in giving you control of the clubhead.

The pressure points in the grip, incidentally, are the middle, ring and little finger of the left hand and the middle and ring finger of the right hand. I've got some pretty sizable callouses there.

STANCE

I'd try to teach people to feel that your toes are up against one side of a railroad track, with the other side of the track being the ball and the clubhead. The tracks are like two parallel lines that never meet. Your feet are aimed just a little bit left of the target.

The feet are set shoulder width apart, the left (or front) foot turned out about 45 degrees, the right (or back) foot just about 90 degrees. The reason for that, of course, is that if you didn't turn the left foot out, the left ankle would block the follow-through, and you couldn't completely turn through the swing. If you have the left foot turned out, that allows the left hip to keep turning a little bit more.

ALIGNMENT

I would teach people that the hips and shoulders should be square to your target, and that the clubhead should be square, too. Basically, from that position the trick is to be able to swing the club back and through a line that would be straight at the target, so you would be hitting down and through that line.

In most cases, beginners don't swing down the line. They swing the clubhead from the outside-in, which causes the slicing motion that is so common. Every now and then, though, I have found a beginner that naturally draws, or hooks, the ball. It's a rare situation, but it has happened.

One thing I do try to relate to young people, or beginners, is my Ping-Pong theory. You know the motion with the paddle that makes the ball curve left or right? Well, the golf club works somewhat the same way. If you can understand the motion done to make the ball curve—turning over the wrist to produce top spin in Ping-Pong is like turning over the golf club to produce a draw—it might help in finding a correction for a problem. Controlling the path of the club-head also enables you to shape your ball flight either right to left or left to right.

POSTURE

I'd talk about the posture in the golf swing by comparing it to standing on the side of a swimming pool, preparing to jump in. You need to have your knees bent slightly.

It's funny, but I have very little knee bend in my set-up. I stand up pretty straight. That has to do with the angle I get between my right forearm and the shaft. It's much a straighter line than the average player, who has a slight angle between the fore-arm and shaft.

One of the biggest problems I see is that at the top of the backswing, the left wrist gets into a bad position. That's because people tend to bend, or cup, their wrist so it's in a weakened position. The left wrist must remain firm and stay in a strong, cocking position.

WEIGHT SHIFT

I would teach players to set up to the ball with 50-50, or even, weight distribution. At the top of the backswing, probably 30 percent of your weight would be on the left (front) side and 70 percent on the right side. At impact, though, the weight has shifted, so that you have 90 percent on the left side and only 10 percent on the right.

The weight shift works down the line of the golf shot. The hips turn through the shot, and you transfer your weight back to the front side. One of the biggest problems for people who slice the golf ball is that they hang back on the right side and don't shift their weight forward. This causes the club to take an outside-in path.

BALANCE

Another problem with slicers is that when they are swinging the club, they keep too much weight back on their heels, which puts them off-balance.

I would teach golfers that balance itself, whether at the address position or the top of the backswing, is pretty important. You need to have your weight balanced over the balls of your feet, in the "ready" athletic position that a linebacker takes in football, where you can move in any direction without falling off-balance one way or another. The best position for hitting a golf ball looks somewhat like a linebacker's stance.

One thing I learned years ago from Jack Barger, a professional in Waco, Texas, was the value of practicing in street shoes or sneakers.

After playing with him, I started doing the same thing, and quickly realized what the benefits are.

For one, street shoes help you maintain your balance throughout the swing. For another, they help you swing within yourself, so you're not overswinging at the ball.

OTHER ADVICE

Another lesson I would teach youngsters, or adult beginners, is that it's okay to go ahead and swing hard at the ball. I think if you taught somebody that the object was to hit the ball in the fairway—and it didn't matter how hard you hit it, just as long as you ended up in the fairway—then, in the long run, when they got to hitting the ball, they would simply hit it short. People who learned the game with that mentality would never attain any distance.

On the other hand, if you took a student and told him, or her, to hit the ball as hard as they can, that player might hit it crazy, or wild, for awhile; but whenever they got a handle on control, they would be hitting the ball really far.

That would be more the approach I would take, to let them go ahead and swing at the ball and hit it hard. I would think that in the long run, that would be beneficial, even though it might not be the easiest way to come about finding a game.

Another important point I would stress to any beginning golfer is this: You cannot learn to play golf on a golf course. The place to learn is on the practice tee, or the driving range (or the schoolyard or city park. Anywhere you have enough room to operate, without hitting balls near joggers or bikers or ballplayers or kite flyers).

The reason you can't learn to play golf on a golf course is that out there, you have to figure out how to survive. How to get the round in, with the least number of mistakes. And you do that by hitting the ball however you have to hit it, to where you're safe and not in trouble. It doesn't matter what flight pattern the ball takes, whether it's high or low, whether it's left to right, or right to left, or whatever. You do what you have to do to get through a round of golf.

One thing I know, on any green there are places you can miss the shot and still have a reasonably good chance of chipping up and taking one putt for par, and there are places you simply cannot miss the shot. If you don't realize the difference, you're going to get in trouble a lot until you do. One thing I've generally been able to do through the years is miss the shot and wind up in the right place, where I'm still playing and still have a chance for par.

I'd also teach beginners how to use the sand wedge. That should be one of the first clubs they start practicing with, simply because I believe you can never be a good player without having a handle on your sand wedge. Not only from 100 yards in, but up around the green, chipping and pitching.

I use a sand wedge, almost invariably, rather than other clubs for little chip shots. I use the sand wedge either for lofted shots or for low running shots, making the adjustment by how I place the blade on the ground and where I put the ball in my stance.

I hood the club to keep the ball low and make it run, and that's the method I would teach any student. One of the main reasons is that you can always hit the ball about the same, and solidly, every time you swing. Otherwise, if you're trying to hit the ball up, maybe with too much wrist action, or hit soft flop shots all the time, the chances of hitting it fat with any club are much, much greater. I would teach someone how to hood the club and hit their chips down and running, where you just loft the ball on to the green and have it running to the hole.

As far as putting goes, I would think the main point to stress is that you don't break your wrists. The wrists must stay very rigid through the putting stroke, to where you never let the face of the putter get ahead of your hands. You do that by keeping the wrists stiff.

PRACTICE

The average golfer devotes little, if any, time to practice. Many golfers never practice. That's why most golfers settle into a handicap within the first couple of years they take up golf and then stay within one or two strokes of that base handicap for the rest of their lives.

The reason so many golfers never improve is that they simply don't work at the game, or practice enough, which is something I cannot comprehend at all. Why would you spend all the money it takes to play golf—for equipment, for green fees, for trips and vacations, for lessons and schools—and then not make a serious effort to play to the best of your ability? That doesn't make any sense to me at all.

I maintain that golfers need to spend at least an equal amount of time practicing—hitting shag balls or range balls, putting and chipping—as they do on the golf course. In my case, I probably spent at least four times as many hours practicing as I ever did playing.

Consequently, my handicap showed constant improvement for years. When I got to Carswell AFB in 1966, I was playing to a 15. By the time I left three years later, my handicap was down to 5. As I've said earlier, I wasn't playing that many rounds of golf each year, but I was putting in hours and hours of practice.

By 1973, when I got really serious about golf, my handicap was down to 1 or 2. And by 1976, when I started shooting my really low rounds—like the 63 at Pecan Valley—my handicap was something like a plus-2. That was probably my best ever, and it was the direct result of serious practice.

> * AND BY 1976, WHEN I STARTED SHOOTING MY REALLY LOW ROUNDS—LIKE THE 63 AT PECAN VALLEY— MY HANDICAP WAS SOMETHING LIKE A PLUS-2.

Granted, practice can be a lonely exercise. It can get wearisome. It's not always fun, but practice does lead to improvement and achievement and produces rewards. Either tangible ones, like trophies, or mental ones, like lowering your handicap.

I can't guarantee that you'll achieve the same sort or results that I have. I will guarantee, however, that anyone who changes some playing hours into practice hours will see his or her handicap go down. It's like Gary Player always says: "The more I practice, the luckier I get."

That brings me to one final point: how to make the most of your practice time. It seems like when the average player does invest a little time in practice, he or she goes to the driving range and hits hard shots with drivers or long clubs. Perhaps all that work on the long game makes them think they're getting more for their money.

They're going about things backward, however. They should be working on the short game, the lofted irons and wedges, because that is where a golfer learns to play the game. In fact, I'd recommend anyone, even a beginner, spend at least 50 percent of each practice session just hitting the sand wedge. That's the one club you're going to have to use at different speeds and different swing tempos.

The sand wedge is really hard to get a handle on, but once you do, it will flow over into every club in the bag. Consequently, you can become a very good player, very quickly, by hitting a lot of balls with sand wedges. They will give you a feel for what it's really like to finesse the ball. This is vital because all good golf revolves around feel.

THE ROBERT LANDERS SCORING SYSTEM

Beginning in 1973, I started keeping a scoring log for

every round of golf I played. I have tried, over the years, to share my system with others. Keith Flatt uses my system, but most people look at me like I'm trying to introduce them to some form of higher mathematics. That's not true at all. My system is really simple. Here's how it works:

To make this system meaningful, you have to put down every round you play, no matter how bad your score. You must play the ball down, resisting the urge to improve your lie. You also must play by the rules of golf. This is hard for some people to do, especially when they get a bad break or a bad lie, but doing so teaches you discipline, and gives you a realistic appraisal of your true ability.

On the top line of the scorecard, I write down my score for each hole, then circle the number, if I reached the green in regulation. On the second line, I put down the number of putts. (Note: Only shots made where the ball is touching the putting surface count as putts.)

I also keep track of the number of times I get up-and-down from off the green, that is, chip up and one-putt. I designate this by X and O, X meaning I wasn't able to; O meaning I was. I count putts from off the green as chips, as well. I put either the X or O symbol on the second line, in the same box as the number of putts.

On the third line of my scorecard, I put the distance of my approach putts. When I reach a green, I immediately step off every putt to get the information to write down on my scorecard (which tells me how close I'm hitting my irons) and to give me some confidence in the putt attempt.

If I sink the putt, I circle the number. At the end of the round, I add up the numbers in the circles, adding one foot to the total distance for each hole that isn't circled. That gives me some standard for consistency, plus accounts for every hole.

The total length of putts made goes into my scoring log. Since I've turned pro, I've started keeping up with how many putts I made under 20 feet, under 10 feet and over 20 feet.

If I chip in from off the green, I don't add that foot. But if I putt the ball in from off the green, I do add the length to the total distance of putts made.

Sometimes, you might stub a shot and have to chip twice on the same hole. In which case, you write more than one symbol in the space for the number of putts. By the way, I only count putts three feet or longer. The ones where you face some stress.

At the bottom of the scorecard, I keep track of how many fairways I hit by using a + or a -. Guess which is which. The other things I keep up with are the number of birdies I make each round (I start with a goal of at least three) and the number of eagles. I log 10 separate items after each round.

I don't separate bunker shots, however. That's because the municipal courses never had many, and the ones that were there I generally avoided.

What my scorecard would tell me is whether, during my next practice session, I should work on driving, iron play, chipping, putting—or maybe all of the above.

The other thing I can do with this information is figure out what constitutes a good, solid round. I know, for example, I need to hit a certain number of fairways (80 percent) and greens (70 percent), in regulation. I know I need a high (66 percent) number of ups-and-downs.

If I reach these little goals, I don't have to worry about big goals. I don't have to worry about success in any one particular tournament, or at any level of play. If I meet these goals, I will be a winner.

COURSE MANAGEMENT

You didn't really expect me to end this chapter on do-it-yourself golf without more preaching on the importance of managing your game on the golf course, did you?

There's a huge difference between hitting golf balls and playing golf. There's also a huge difference between having a good golf swing and being a player.

The first thing a player has to do is figure out how to play some percentages. By that I mean, on every shot you have to reach some decision as to what club to use and what kind of shot to play to give yourself the best chance for success. In other words, you have to turn the percentages in your favor. If you don't, you'll never be able to play consistent golf.

You base these decisions on distance and direction. By knowing how far you hit the ball with each of your clubs, and knowing whether you fade, draw or hit your shots straight, you can determine the best place to miss the target, if it's not going to be your best shot.

Once you recognize where you can miss a shot—and where you can't—and you know your game well enough to avoid the trouble, you will begin to change the percentages in your favor. And you'll be well on the way to playing real golf and to being a real golfer.

For example, when I was learning to play at golf courses like Rockwood, Pecan Valley and Z. Boaz, I always tried to hit my approach shots between the front of the green and the pin. I seldom tried to hit the ball to the pin, or past the pin. Why? Because playing to the front of the green left me with uphill putts, which are easier than downhill putts. And there was less trouble in front of the greens, which were open, than on the sides or back of the greens, which often were guarded by bunkers.

THE CARDINAL SINS

One way I recommend that you learn to play golf is by avoiding what I call the "three cardinal sins" of golf, which many high-handicap players frequently commit. All golfers should try to adopt this philosophy.

ONE WAY I RECOMMEND THAT YOU LEARN TO PLAY GOLF IS BY AVOIDING WHAT I CALL THE "THREE CARDINAL SINS."

One, *never make double-bogeys.* Those are what eat a hole in the scorecard. You can eliminate double-bogeys in a hurry by learning to how to use your sand wedge and developing a feel for playing shots from 100 yards in. Especially those chips and pitches around the green. If you're going to lose strokes to par, do so one at a time.

Two, *avoid penalty strokes.* Make a plan for playing each golf course that minimizes your exposure to hazards or out-of-bounds stakes. Play within yourself and don't try to attempt shots that aren't in your bag.

Three, *avoid three-putt greens.* The best way to manage that, of course, is to practice your long putting. Concentrate on developing a feel for the speed of long putts. Even if you miss the intended line slightly, you'll still wind up somewhere near the hole.

I would tell any golf student that he or she would be pleasantly surprised how fast they'll start trimming strokes off their scores by eliminating double-bogeys, penalty strokes and three-putt greens.

Good luck. With hard work, dedication to practice, goal-setting and some sound thinking on the golf course, I'm certain you'll be shooting better scores in no time at all.

GREENER
PASTURES

Epilogue

At the Cadillac NFL Golf Classic in Clifton, New Jersey on May 12-14, Robert Landers posted his best finish yet on the 1995 Senior PGA Tour. He shot rounds of 71-75-74/220 (4 over), tying for 34th. He earned his largest weekly paycheck to date: $5,266.

After the tournament, Landers flew from Newark to Tyler, Texas, to participate in the Eisenhower International Golf Classic, a pro-am at Willow Brook Country Club that annually attracts golf fans from all over East Texas and contestants from as far away as Vermont.

He shot 70, one-under par. His amateur team, consisting of local businessmen Bennett White, Lynn Acker, Mike Paxson and Larry Williams, shot 19-under par. After the round, Landers gave interviews to local TV and radio stations and signed autographs for members of the Moo Crew.

He also signed legal documents for the creation of Robert Landers Golf, Inc., a direct marketing golf equipment company that will sell custom-designed Robert Landers golf clubs featuring an Adams Air Assault head and a Holstein-patterned black-and-white super shaft, like Landers uses in competition on the Senior PGA Tour.

The clubs will be designed and manufactured by Barney Adams of Adams Golf in Dallas, whose Adams Air Assault woods and irons that have been finding their way into some famous bags on the Senior PGA Tour, including Lee Trevino's and Rocky Thompson's. Initial production runs will include 46" and 48" drivers (Landers himself uses the former) and a 3-wood, 5-wood and 7-wood.

Robert Landers Golf, Inc. will be based in Mineral Wells, Texas. Landers' partners in the venture are Jerry Hamilton and E.A. Connel, a Mineral Wells businessman. The company also plans to market Robert Landers-branded golf balls, tees, caps and head covers. There is a toll-free telephone number, 1-800-MOO-CREW, for customer use and convenience, and an infomercial is being considered.

On Monday evening, May 15, Robert and Freddie Landers were reunited at Dallas/Fort Worth International Airport. They flew to Philadelphia for the Bell Atlantic Classic. Before the tournament began, Robert Landers played in a benefit for the Sertoma Club and got in a practice round at one of America's most famous golf courses, Pine Valley.

Robert Landers' amazing golf saga—his incredible journey from a Texas farm to the green pastures of the professional tour—continues.

GREENER
PASTURES

A special thanks to our contributing photographers, Michael O'Bryon and Scott Halleran. Kudos to Park Van Nest, Pam Dodson, and Joe Grubbs for their relentless effort to seeing this project to completion.